INFORMATION SYSTEMS FOR MANAGERS
Casebook

D1825683

CARL R. RUTHSTROM, PH.D.
Associate Professor of Management

CHARLENE A. DYKMAN, PH.D.
Associate Professor of Computer Information Systems

WEST PUBLISHING COMPANY
St. Paul   New York   Los Angeles   San Francisco

Cover image: "Efforts for Affection," detail of hand silkscreen printed cotton. Copyright © 1990 by Dawn Zero Erickson, courtesy of the Kyoto Textile Resource Museum, Kyoto, Japan. Photographed by Daniel A. Erickson.

WEST'S COMMITMENT TO THE ENVIRONMENT
In 1906, West Publishing Company began recycling materials left over from the production of books. This began a tradition of efficient and responsible use of resources. Today, up to 95% of our legal books and 70% of our college texts are printed on recycled, acid-free stock. West also recycles nearly 22 million pounds of scrap paper annually—the equivalent of 181,717 trees. Since the 1960s, West has devised ways to capture and recycle waste inks, solvents, oils, and vapors created in the printing process. We also recycle plastics of all kinds, wood, glass, corrugated cardboard, and batteries, and have eliminated the use of styrofoam book packaging. We at West are proud of the longevity and the scope of our commitment to our environment.

Production, Prepress, Printing and Binding by West Publishing Company.

CONTENTS

Case   **Title/Description**

The objectives of this case are to allow students to explore what appears to be a complex ethics related situation, solve the immediate issue of completing the in-progress roofing job on time, and then move on to a more permanent long term solution by developing the framework for a purchasing, production control, and inventory management system.

This case traces the development of an image processing system for the Automobile Club of Southern California. The Club entered into a strategic alliance with IBM for this project. The organizational impacts are presented for analysis.

With deregulation, the bank's traditional way of making money, the "spread" between the interest rate it paid depositors and the interest rate it charged borrowers, was drastically reduced. Thus, they began to search for other strategies to maintain and improve profit levels. Southern National had bought, created or spun off a number of subsidiaries in the area of fee-for-services and other quasi-banking businesses.

The board of directors found 16 out of 18 of the subsidiaries showing losses. The Board of Directors fired the previous Chairman, appointed a new Chairman, and demanded immediate action.

This case allows students to identify product differences and similarities between computer workstations and personal computers as well as target markets and promising applications of each type. It permits students to evaluate growth and profitability strategies employed by Sun Microsystems and IBM, to consider alternatives, and to recommend programs and policies in view of changing competitive environments.

A systems analyst has been asked to examine the current operations of the County Ambulance Service. The demand for the service has grown substantially in the past ten years and is expected to double over the next five years. Due to this growth, the information gathering, communication, and coordination have deteriorated. The systems analyst is expected to make recommendations for improvements including identification of criteria and standards for evaluation of the various components of the system.

This set of three minicases illustrates the dilemmas in managing the end-user computing area within an organization. A distributed system to be used by insurance agents presents some interesting dilemmas. A computer-assisted dispatching system for a police department and an energy conservation system, both off-the-shelf software, are discussed.

Work groups that experience basic technological change must address many issues in their efforts to adapt. This case deals with the implementation of a computer-based messaging system for international communications and the need to consider the entire work system, including the people, groups, and work processes that are affected, in order to successfully implement such systems.

Advances in technology now allow hotel operators to "remember" every guest's preferences through guest histories. However, few hotels are making use of the mountain of data that guests leave behind. Using new technology to manage guest information and restore the "personal touch" provides managers with a competitive edge.

As small computers increased processing capabilities and storage capacities on a par with mainframes, downsizing of computer hardware systems continues unabated. Many mainframe users were switching to networks of mini- and micro-computers. IBM was faced with the need to reorient their product lines and their sales and service organizations without seriously damaging employee morale, customer service levels, and organizational continuity.

Many end-user manuals are still being written without regard for the non-technical end-user. This case illustrates why more care needs to be taken in writing manuals which end-users use in operation of their systems. The case shows the problems and frustration encountered by a pharmacist interacting with a system during work hours and reiterates the need for readable procedures for the end-user.

The purpose of this case study is to highlight traditional departmental differences in acquisition and implementation of information processing tools. An international electronic messaging system has created friction between the administrative services and information systems departments. The importance of the systems development life cycle becomes apparent through an analysis of a failed implementation.

Krueper Engineering is having difficulty making the transition to a Stage 2 firm. It has grown beyond the stage where one person can be involved in all aspects of the business. The firm's greatest asset still runs the firm as if it were a 15-person enterprise. In some areas the owner has delegated responsibilities, but in other areas he has relinquished very little control. The net result is a firm with an outstanding reputation for thoroughness of its reports struggling with a high stress overload due to a six months backlog of work.

This case deals with the problems created by a merger. The newly hired Fleet Manager must integrate two fleets of trucks into a single entity. The one fleet has experienced high operating costs, a good safety record and high driver retention. The other fleet has significantly reduced operating costs through a transportation improvement program (TRIM) which includes the use of on-board computerized trip recorders. Countering the reduced operating costs is a 40 percent turnover rate of drivers. This case involves a unique MIS application, data security, privacy of information, and labor relations.

LCTX faces a turbulent environment with rapidly changing technology, governmental regulations, customer demands, and increased competition. This case discusses the issues involved in making optimal computing hardware decisions that will position the company for profitability, stability, flexibility and growth in this dynamic environment.

This case involves moving from a monopolistic mind-set to one that is market driven. The unifying concept is that improving the quality of customer service leads to competitive advantage. The issues include deregulation, new technologies, competition, changing the corporate culture, and the new measurement and control systems required to enable the company to achieve its goals.

Vacbag is a subsidiary of the Consolidated Vacuum Company and an industry leader in the innovation, design, and manufacture of heavy duty vacuum accessories. Vacbag's President has initiated a major effort to integrate advanced office automation technology into the company in an effort to increase productivity and the company's competitive advantage. Numerous managerial issues provide the basis for analysis and discussion of a major office automation project.

Southern Utility was using telecommunications networking facilities for data communications in support of an information system supporting 2,500 on-line terminals. Management has just approved a program to add another 1,800 more terminals to the same network. An effective management strategy must be developed to evaluate and control the sizing, sequencing, timing, and costs of the program.

The information technology group enables United State Insurers (USI) to provide superior claim service and to offer insurance products targeted to many income groups. However, the delivery of these strategically important information products has become problematic. A consulting company studied the project team organization and recommended a new organization for better use of human resources. The new organization was implemented and is causing new problems.

Sun Microsystems is facing intense competition from the mid-range computer manufacturers, IBM, DEC, and Hewlett Packard, as well as personal computer manufacturers, Compaq, Apple, Sony, and others. Sun must decide which of its multiple goals have the highest priority, and allocate its product design, production, marketing, and financial resources accordingly.

Systematics, a financial services company, faces many internally and externally generated problems and opportunities. Acquired by ALLTEL Corporation in 1990, Systematics has suddenly obtained access to a vast amount of capital to pursue additional growth avenues. The President of Systematics must deal with the disruptive changes occurring in the banking industry. The massive consolidations and mergers have affected Systematics as a major supplier of software and other financial services.

The case focuses on the evaluation of computer alternatives, the options for a firm in a declining market, more effective financial decision-making for the future, and the issue of managerial competency. There are serious management problems which the owners feel can be alleviated with the purchase of a computer system. The financial difficulties have occurred as a result of family rivalries.

The case brings to life a company that has been using information technology not only to change its internal operations and its products, but to also change its market. The Chief Information Officer is a key player in strategic planning and acts as the "bridge" or "great communicator" between the IT unit and the other functional units in the company. The risks of this strategy become clear during a three week absence of the CIO.

A small worker-owned and operated business has a goal of serving the community with nutritious, natural baked goods while creating fulfilling jobs for its employees. Growth threatens the personal, informal structure which the owners value highly. The new role, as a supplier to various supermarkets, is compelling the business to adopt a more formalized organizational structure with a high technology orientation. This has added a computer systems analyst whose specialized position creates friction and resentment among other key employees.

We gratefully acknowledge the case research and writing of the authors who contributed their cases to this book. The wide breadth of topics covered by these cases is the cumulative experience of over twenty "real" organizations researched by the authors. We want to thank Susan Smart, our editor for guiding us through this project. We are grateful to our assistants, Bridgett Carroll and Tahirah Waits, who used part of their Christmas holiday to assist us in typing and formatting the book. Last, but not least, we give special thanks to our spouses, Dolores Ruthstrom and Charles Davis, for their understanding and support as we attempted to meet very short deadlines.

Case Authors

Name/Affiliation   **Case Numbers**

CHAPTER 1
INTRODUCTION

Information Systems for Managers, 2nd Edition, by George W. Reynolds, presents a wide range of technologies and methodologies that are associated with the field of Management Information Systems. It is a book that is intended to position business managers to make effective decisions regarding the use of these technologies and methodologies in their own functional areas. Information systems are a resource for the organization that chooses to use them. They should bring real benefit to that host organization.

In the 1990s, it is clear that computing technology will no longer be isolated in the back room of the data center. The competitive stance of business organizations of the future will depend, in large measure, on that organization's ability to make effective use of computing technology to increase productivity, lower costs, and gain strategic advantage. In order to achieve these ends, the organization's knowledge of the fundamentals of computing technology and familiarity with the information systems industry will be required. The ability to make financially and strategically sound decisions with respect to I.S. technology will determine the success of the company. Such decisions, in many cases, will be made by students in today's university classes.

Information Systems for Managers: Casebook is designed to offer students of business an opportunity to become involved with real-world situations describing the development and operation of information systems. The student will make decisions regarding the people, money, and equipment associated with the rapidly changing world of information systems.

You may be expected, as a business employee, to use information technology at many stages of your work process. As a manager, you will be held accountable for the

1

expenditures you approve in your areas. You will also be held accountable for making optimal use of technological advances that may address work process issues in your area of responsibility. Both levels of employees will spend time working with the information systems staff to address automation issues that impact their functional areas.

Thorough analysis of these cases will be beneficial in helping you understand the hidden issues and the subtle nuances that must be considered to make a good decision about the technology or organizational issues involved. Such analysis will also prepare you for building a solid foundation for the high-quality and intelligent decision-making that will be needed to survive in the highly competitive environment of the 1990's.

Information Systems for Managers: Casebook offers many kinds of cases that address various areas of the information technology profession. You will need to consider whether new technology is worth the expense. You will be asked to evaluate the potential viability of various technologies. If you decide to implement a new system, will it still be supported in ten years? If not, what does that mean to your firm? You will consider various ways to structure the information systems capability of the firm. You will be asked to think about ways to deploy information technology and its associated methodologies and procedures for the competitive advantage of the firm.

In sum, this casebook is compiled to give the business student real-world situations with which to become involved. These cases will take you out of the basic information about a particular technology and into the use of that technology for the benefit of the firm. You will be asked to make the decisions and to consider the issues that bridge the gap between the technology and its real-world business application. All of this is offered to the reader from the perspective of the business advantages to be gained from the use of the technology.

The cases are matched with the appropriate chapters in Information Systems for Managers by George Reynolds. It should be noted that some cases are listed under more than one chapter. For example, "Lewis Foods Fleet Management (B)" contains issues involving applications, implementation, human factors, data security and privacy.

CHAPTER REFERENCE MATRIX

CHAPTER	PRIMARY CASE(S)	SECONDARY CASE(S)
1. Management & IS Technology	#7	#2, #15, #23
2. Management Perspective of IS	#7, #5	#15
3. Computer Hardware & Software	#4, #9, #14, #19	#17
4. Networks	#12, #22, #17	#3, #8, #12
5. Data Management	#8, #1	#5, #6, #13, #22
6. Applications	#3, #15, #22	#5, #6 #13, #19
7. System Development Methodology & CASE	#11	#10, #16
8. Defining the IS Strategic Plan	#12, #20, #22	#3, #8, #14, #23
9. Steering the Application Development Process	#10	#11
10. Acquiring IS Resources	#2. #20, #21	#7, #11, #14
11. End-User Computing & Information Centers	#6, #10, #16	#7
12. Managing IS Professionals	#18, #23	#6
13. Computer Security & Disaster Planning		#12, #13
14. Critical Issues Facing CIOs	#12, #13, #20	#9, #15, #22

ISSUES REFERENCE MATRIX

ISSUE	PRIMARY CASE(S)	SECONDARY CASE(S)
Planning	#17, #23	#7
Using Consultants	#21	#17, #22
Privacy	#13	#8
IS Dept. Structure	#22	
Org. Impact of Systems	#6, #7	#10, #18, #22
Strategic Alliances	#2	#9, #19
Role of IS Dept.	#6, #12	#18, #23
Human Factors	#12, #13, #18, #23	#10, #16
Distributed Processing	#8, #16	
Mainframe vs. PCs	#9	#22
Purchased Software		#6
Impact of Deregulation	#15	#3, #14
Quality Assurance	#22, #15	#5
User Training	#9	
Disaster/Recovery	#12	#22
Mergers/Acquisitions	#13, #20	#4
Growth Management	#12, #23	#4, #5, #9, #18
Coping with Competition	#3, #8, #12, #15, #22	#2, #9
Changing Marketplace	#4, #9, #15, #18	#8, #23
Projects behind Schedule	#1, #12, #15	#4, #18
Organizational Politics	#11	#9, #23
Job Design	#18	#2, #10
System Obsolescence	#8, #16	

TECHNOLOGY REFERENCE MATRIX

TECHNOLOGY	PRIMARY CASE(S)	SECONDARY CASE(S)
Image Processing	#2	
Distributed DBMS	#18, #22	#8
Mainframes	#9	#22
Personal Computers	#6	#9, #19
Dispatching Systems	#6	#5
Energy Conservation Systems	#6	
Database	#8, #22, #1	
Documentation	#10	
Networks	#17, #22	#12
Cellular Phones/Comm. Services		#20
Banking Systems	#3, #20	#19
Bar Coding	#23	
Work Measurement Sys.	#13, #15	
Workstations	#4, #12	
Materials Mgt. Sys.	#22	
Distribution Sys.	#22	#18
Telex Systems	#7	
Mid-Range Computers	#4, #9, #12, #14	
Development Methods	#11	#16
End-User Computing	#6	#9, #10
Electronic Data Interchange Systems	#22	
Electronic Mail	#11	

CASE 1
A-1 ROOFING COMPANY[1]

A-1 Roofing's marketing manager had just completed a telephone call informing one of A-1 Roofing's customers that the roofing job on their buildings was delayed due to a shortage of roofing cement. He could remember word for word the customer's angry reaction to the news.

"I have already made commitments for the building to be leased," the customer hissed. "I warn you that, if the deadline for completion is missed, I will invoke the penalty clauses in the contract. These clauses allow me to recoup any lost rent revenues and $300 per day for each day the project is late."

The marketing manager had heard that purchasing had encountered an ethics problem with one of their vendors. He wondered if this were the case or if a severe management problem existed in Purchasing? Before he approached the president of A-1 Roofing Company he knew that he needed more facts about the shortage of roofing cement.

Background

A-1 Roofing Company, a small construction company, specialized in installing and repairing the roofs of commercial buildings. The company had never roofed

---

[1] This case, written by Carl R. Ruthstrom, University of Houston-Downtown, is based on field research by John E. Geydos, a Purchasing and Materials Management major. Published with the permission of the North American Case Research Association.

residential buildings. The company prided itself in providing quality roof installation and repair in a timely manner. They accomplished this by hiring skilled employees and giving them the authority to carry out their jobs with minimum intervention by upper management.

Chris Moore, the Purchasing Manager for A-1 Roofing, had recently retired. Unknown to upper management, Chris Moore relied heavily on his best friend, Gary Weddle, to make many of his purchasing decisions. Gary was a roofing expert employed as a salesman with Gardner Bender Roofing Products. Chris and Gary had been friends for years and frequently went on fishing trips together. This unique relationship enabled Gardner Bender to receive numerous purchase orders for roofing supplies from A-1 Roofing.

Of all the applicants for the position of Purchasing Manager, Clyde Lair was the only person with previous construction buying experience. He had lost his last job when the home builder that employed him went out of business. Clyde was the lumber and hardware buyer for the home builder and had no background in buying roofing materials. During his employment interview, Clyde stated that he had been able to issue purchase orders for up to $50,000 without prior approval from upper management. The interviewer made no comment about this approval limit. A-1 Roofing hired Clyde on the basis that his previous construction experience would enable him to easily learn the roofing business.

Once he started to work, Clyde discovered that the management style of A-1 Roofing was "laissez faire." When he asked for a company policy manual, he was told that employees were hired for their expertise and were expected to use their best judgement to help make the company profitable. He was also told that the company viewed him as a professional and would respect his judgement on matters regarding the purchasing department.

Current Situation

Shortly after accepting the position of Purchasing Manager at A-1 Roofing, Clyde was notified that an existing contract had been expanded to include several more buildings. Although this was A-1 Roofing's busiest season, marketing had agreed to a short completion date because the added buildings were in the vicinity of the work already in progress.

Clyde immediately called Brian Disney, the Warehouse Manager, to insure that adequate materials were available for the added work. Brian informed Clyde there was no more roofing cement in stock - all of the previous stock had been sent to the job site. Several weeks earlier, Brian had notified Chris that the supply of roofing cement was low. Chris had been preoccupied with his retirement plan and failed to order more roofing cement.

When questioned about the type of cement A-1 Roofing used, Brian told Clyde that the new roofs were being installed with a roofing cement called Gardner Bender. The only thing Brian could remember was that the cement buckets had a yellow label.

After checking previous purchase orders, Clyde found several purchase orders for Gardner Bender Roofing Cement-Yellow Label. Clyde also located a spiral notebook marked Approved Vendors-Products. Stapled to the top of each page of the notebook was a business card of a salesman. Below the business card were brief descriptions of the products sold by the salesman's company. On one page, Clyde found a business card for Gary Weddle, a salesman for Gardner Bender. On the same page, was an entry for Gardner Bender Roofing Cement-Yellow Label.

Clyde checked the contract for the job in progress and found that the only requirement for the roofing cement was "one that meets commercial code applications." There was no mention of brand names and no specifications attached to the contract.

At this point, Clyde contacted Gardner Bender. He was informed that Gary Weddle was on vacation and that Danny Turner, another sales representative, would help him. Danny, a recent college graduate, had only been employed by Gardner Bender for three weeks.

Clyde explained that he was not familiar with the products that had been ordered by A-1 Roofing in the past, but from old purchase orders, he had found the product, Gardner Bender Roofing Cement-Yellow Label. Danny searched through his sales literature and located roofing cements. A picture on the page showed a can of roofing cement with a yellow label on it. What Danny did not realize was that not all of the products listed on the page had a corresponding picture.

Assuming that this was the correct cement, Danny provided a quote of $27,000 for the quantity Clyde wanted to order. Clyde placed a purchase order for the cement. Following the format of the previous purchase orders, Clyde described the product as Gardner Bender Roofing Cement-Yellow Label.

Several days later, the shipment arrived at A-1 Roofing's warehouse. The receiving personnel checked the quantity and description on the purchase order against the packing slip and the merchandise. They were satisfied that the correct quantity was received and that the containers were Gardner Bender Roofing Cement-Yellow Label. The purchase order, receiver, and packing slip were forwarded to accounting. The merchandise was sent to the warehouse.

The warehouse personnel did not have enough storage area inside the building to accommodate the entire shipment. Approximately one-third of the order was stored in an outside area enclosed by an eight feet chain link fence. For the next several days, these containers were subjected to intense heat during the day and rain during the night.

When the roofing cement was finally sent to the job site, the foreman at the site recognized that the cement was not the same consistency as that previously used. Upon reading the label, the foreman discovered that the last shipment was for aluminum roofs, not for the composition roof on which they were working. He immediately called Clyde to inform him of the error. The work was stopped and the roofing crew had to be sent home with pay for the entire day. The subcontract with this crew stipulated that they would be paid for the entire day if they were sent home for any reason other than inclement weather.

Clyde called Gardner Bender. Fortunately, Gary was back from vacation. Gary agreed to allow the cement to be returned, but he explained there was a 20% restocking fee on all returned merchandise. His agreement was also on the condition that the cans were unopened and in the same condition as when they were delivered.

Clyde was angry. He insisted that there would be no restocking fee because Danny, not A-1 Roofing, had made the error. Danny should have known that the cement was for aluminum roofs and should have questioned if the product were to be used for aluminum roofs. Clyde also insisted that Danny should have checked previous shipment records to see what had been supplied in the past. Gary referred the matter to his sales manager. The sales manager would not budge; to him, policy was policy. The sales manager also added the stipulation that A-1 Roofing would have to pay for the transportation costs of the return to Gardner Bender. The sales manager's position was that A-1 Roofing had asked for and had received yellow label cement.

Gary thought he could resolve this issue more easily if he went to A-1 Roofing personally. Upon arrival at the warehouse, Gary discovered the portion that was stored outside. The cans were rusty from the rain. Gary informed Clyde that not only were the previous stipulations still in effect, but that the cans stored outside could not be returned. He pointed out that the label clearly stated to store the cans in a cool dry area. Gary was not sure of any damage to the cement other than the appearance of the cans.

Clyde referred the matter to the president of A-1 Roofing. The president notified the accounting department to withhold payment to Gardner Bender until the matter was resolved. An agreement was finally reached late Friday afternoon. Gardner Bender agreed to lower the restocking fee to five percent if A-1 Roofing would apply the full refund towards the purchase of the correct roofing cement. A-1 Roofing was still responsible for the transportation costs of the return shipment and none of the cans stored outside were to be shipped back to Gardner Bender.

After the agreement was reached, Clyde was informed by Gary that Gardner Bender did not have enough of the required cement in stock to fill the entire order. But the real dilemma was that this Friday, the day of the agreement, Gardner Bender would begin its annual two-week plant shutdown. Only maintenance and inventory personnel would be at the plant for the next two weeks.

Reluctantly, Clyde notified the Marketing Manager of the problem. The Marketing Manager then informed the customer of the delay and immediately started investigating the problem.

Conclusion

A-1 Roofing's Marketing manager had just completed his review of the current problem of the "Yellow-Label" roofing cement. He knew that the customer's angry reaction to the news that the roofing jobs would be at least two weeks late was no idle threat. The marketing manager knew that he had to develop some alternatives before he approached the president for help in resolving the following questions:

(1)   How to complete the job in progress within the time specified in the contract?

(2)   How to insure that the correct materials were ordered by Purchasing?

(3)   How to prevent the repetition of this incident on another roofing cement order or any other commodity that A-1 Roofing uses?

EXERCISE

From a systems management viewpoint complete the following:

1.   Assist the Marketing Manager in developing a short-term solution to the problem by developing an answer for each of his questions.

2.   List the database files needed by A-1 Roofing and the contents of each.

3.   Design a flow chart or data flow diagram for the computerized information system showing the inputs and outputs needed to communicate effectively in A-1 Roofing's materials management system.

CASE 2
AUTOMOBILE CLUB OF SOUTHERN CALIFORNIA[1]

In July 1990, Tom McKernan, Executive Vice President and Chief Financial Officer of the Automobile Club of Southern California (ACSC) reflected on the status of the image processing project, which was one year into its projected four year schedule. Thus far, the project was proceeding according to schedule, with the installation of a new mainframe, optical storage drives and 64 image workstations in the Costa Mesa Processing Center.

Looking for ways to reduce the enormous amount of paper handling in the Auto Club's insurance business (over 30,000 pieces per day), Tom believed that image processing, the ability to electronically (or optically) store and retrieve documents in image form, would enable the Club to reduce costs and improve customer service. With over 25 years experience in information systems Tom, previously Director of Data Processing, convinced the Club's Board of Directors to commit $6 million dollars to this project, with an expected saving of $2 million dollars a year after 1993.

Once imaging streamlined the policy side of the insurance business, Tom felt this same technology could be used in claims processing. This area relied quite heavily on externally generated documents, such as medical reports, legal depositions, and bills. Other Auto Club services, such as travel, and road service also might benefit. Tom realized that making a large commitment to this new technology assumed considerable risk, but felt that the potential competitive advantage tipped the scales in favor of the project.

---

[1] This case was written by Wendy K. Wanderman and Steven S. Curl, California State Polytechnic University, Pomona, and Sidney E. Harris, Peter F. Drucker Management Center, The Claremont Graduate School.

Company Background

The Automobile Club of Southern California was founded in December 1900. Initially composed of ten members, ACSC was chartered as a not-for-profit association "for persons either owning or having an interest in self-propelled vehicles." In the years to follow, the Auto Club grew at an astounding rate with growth being reflected in the number of new members as well as member services. Affiliated with the American Automobile Association (AAA), the Auto Club of Southern California was the acknowledged leader in the motor club arena, controlling about 65% of the market in 1989. However, formidable competition existed; most notable among these were Allstate Motor Club, Montgomery Ward Auto Club, Amoco Motor Club, Exxon Travel Club, Chevron, and Mobil.

ACSC had never wavered in its efforts to provide first class service to its members and in its strong commitment to public service. Best known for its Emergency Road Service (ERS), the Club had been instrumental in many other areas, including the charting, engineering, and signposting of thousands of miles of roads and highways and legislative lobbying for improved motor vehicle laws. In fact, the ACSC wrote the first California motor vehicle code in the 1920's.

By 1989, ACSC served 3.5 million members and provided insurance for 1 million automobiles and 50,000 homes. Principal member services included: emergency road service; new vehicle financing; automobile, boat, and homeowner insurance; Department of Motor Vehicle registration services; travel-related services, such as touring information, reservations, ticketing, cruises, tours, maps, and travelers checks; hunting and fishing licenses; international driving permits; and traffic citation services. Additionally, the Auto Club continued to review and initiate legislation benefitting the motorist.

The Club Facilities

The Club's facilities consisted of its Los Angeles Headquarters, the Costa Mesa Processing Center, and 79 district offices located throughout Southern California. In 1990, the Club had 5,600 employees serving the membership and insurance needs of its 3.6 million members.

ACSC Headquarters

The Club's Headquarters occupied an enclave of Spanish styled buildings, near the University of Southern California, in downtown Los Angeles. This facility, a registered cultural historical landmark, housed the underwriting staff, claims administration, executive offices, emergency road service (ERS) administration, travel services administration and legal division, as well as a full-service district office to serve its members who lived and/or worked in the downtown area. In 1990, 1,200 employees worked at Headquarters.

Costa Mesa Processing Center

The Costa Mesa Processing Center (CMPC) opened in 1982 to serve the processing needs of the Club's member services and insurance operation. CMPC's primary functions included: providing administrative and operating support for membership and insurance transactions; recording financial information and producing legally required information needed for reporting purposes; and providing support of direct member services through a modern, complex telecommunications network.

CMPC, with its advanced computer and telecommunications system, handled all the processing needs of Headquarters and each of the 79 district offices spread over the 13 Southern California counties. The Emergency Road Service (ERS) center for Orange county was also located here. This facility received the 'Office of the Year' Award of Merit for 1983 by Office Administration and Automation (OAA) magazine. In presenting the award, OAA paid tribute to the fact that the Club designed the facility to provide a smooth work flow, while at the same time "creating a pleasing environment for its employees." In 1990, it housed 1,200 employees.

District Offices

The Auto Club provided high-quality services to its members through a network of 79 district offices located throughout the 13 Southern California counties. Its northern-most office was in San Luis Obispo. Permitting members ready access to Auto Club services was one of the Club's goals.

A full service district office offered extensive travel agency services in addition to the roadmap and AAA reservation services. Claims adjusters were assigned to the district offices to provide better customer service in claims settlements and insurance assessments. District offices also worked with local communities, to provide information on travel-related issues, including public safety and crime prevention.

The Club's Insurance Services

The Club initiated a separate entity to sell automobile insurance in the State of California in 1912 as a reciprocal interinsurance exchange. Such an exchange could only sell insurance to its members; profits were returned to the members through dividends and reduced premiums. The Club's Board of Directors was persuaded to start an insurance operation because, with automobile ownership still in its infancy, most insurance companies had not yet offered this type of coverage. The Club viewed auto insurance as an extension of its many other motoring services. Over the years, it extended its insurance offerings to include: watercraft, recreational vehicles, and residential real estate (homeowner's).

The Effects of Government Regulations

The 1980's saw automobile insurance costs skyrocket. Explanations for this rapid escalation in costs included a more litigious society, larger settlement costs, increased fraud, and the cost of complying with increasing government regulations. Prior to the 1980's, many people had considered customer service to be an important component in selecting insurance coverage; as the cost of carrying insurance increased, consumers began to view the product more as a commodity. Low cost became an equal, if not more important, consideration compared with service. The market became extremely price sensitive and insurance carriers were pressured to cut costs and increase profitability. Costs in the industry were determined primarily by claim payments, underwriting expenses, claims processing, and policy administration.

With its geographically dispersed population and a lack of adequate public transportation, many Southern California residents found themselves depending on the automobile as the only viable means of getting to and from work. Combined with the rapid escalation in automobile insurance rates, this left many working poor unable to afford the cost of insurance. Consequently, those people simply drove uninsured, causing a public outcry which resulted in the State of California mandating that all automobile drivers must carry liability insurance. An assigned risk pool was created for those drivers whose poor driving record prevented them from obtaining their own auto insurance; all insurance companies licensed to do business in the State were required to accept a certain percentage of these policies, which were assigned at random.

With increasing government intervention, the insurance industry became increasingly politicized. Proposition 103, which became law in November 1988, was only one example of this trend. Proposition 103 mandated: (1) that all insurance carriers conform to a common rating system as specified by statute; (2) the commissioner of insurance would be an elected position (it had been a gubernatorial appointment); and (3) a rate rollback of 20% below 1987 levels. In sharp response to this, many insurance carriers challenged the legality of the proposition's reforms in court, while others threatened to simply leave the California insurance market.

Much of the debate centered around that portion of the proposition permitting insurers to earn a "fair" rate of return. Rate increases were to be approved by the Insurance Commissioner according to this standard. If the Commissioner disagreed with the carriers, the issue was settled by the courts. The result was increased volatility and uncertainty in the industry as well as increased litigation costs. Unlike several insurance companies who refused to follow the new rules until specific regulations were issued, ACSC made the required adjustments and reporting changes. According to Rich Revell, Director of Data Processing and Systems, it took 21 man-years of programmer/analyst time to make all the necessary system changes to conform with the new regulations.

The changing regulatory and competitive environment had an especially hard impact on the Club. Unlike some of its competitors, its geographical territory was limited to Southern California. As the cost of doing business in Southern California (and especially in Los Angeles County) increased, the Auto Club's insurance rates became less competitive. By 1990, the percentage of the members purchasing their insurance through the Auto Club declined to about 20%. Club membership had grown rapidly while the insurance service grew more slowly or even declined in some years.

In accordance with California's mandatory insurance law, the Auto Club, which had entered the insurance business intending to provide insurance only to its members, found itself forced to insure an increasing number of (non-member) assigned risk drivers. The number of these policies rose dramatically from 14,000 in 1988 to 63,000 by the end of 1989. By 1990, assigned risk policies accounted for approximately 9% of the Club's written premium policies. Rates for assigned risk drivers were set by the State and, in 1989, were insufficient to cover the cost of the policies. Accordingly, the net loss incurred from insuring these drivers was born by all insured drivers. According to Al Bailey, Director of Administrative Services, approximately $65 of every car's insurance premium subsidized the cost of carrying the assigned risk policies. It was imperative that the Club find ways to significantly reduce the costs related to its insurance business.

Competitive Environment

During the 1980's, the insurance portion of ACSC's business faced stiff competition. Some of the major competitors were Allstate, Farmers, Mercury, State Farm, and 20th Century. Between 1982 and 1989, the Club's market share had fallen from 11.8% to 6.6%.

For the period 1982 through 1987, ACSC's net written premiums grew at a compound annual rate of 6.8%. By comparison, other carriers of auto insurance (Allstate, CSAA, Farmers, Mercury, State Farm, and 20th Century) grew at an annualized rate ranging from 11.6% (Farmers) to 36.7% (Mercury). The net result of these relative growth rates had been a decline in the Club's share of the market. The Club was not alone in experiencing a decline in market share; the other major carriers (Allstate, Farmers, and State Farm) experienced declines as well.

Some of the firms experiencing the greatest increase in market share were new entrants in the market that only sold their policies through direct mail solicitation. By not maintaining a field operations network, these carriers had lower overall operating costs. As a group, the Auto Club, Allstate, Farmers, and State Farm lost a combined 15.3% of their market; the direct mail marketers experienced an 119% increase in market share during this same period.

Application Processing

As with other services, the sale of insurance was handled through the district offices. Members could apply for insurance at any district office. The forms were complicated, so a trained staff member completed them for the member. The staff was responsible for seeing that the paperwork was completed correctly and also for verifying the condition of the automobile. The member paid 25% of the estimated annual premium when applying for the policy. One copy of the application was routed to the Los Angeles facility for underwriting approval, one copy was retained at the member's district office, and a third copy was kept by the member.

Once the Auto Club's representative accepted the member's application, the applicant was covered while the application was processed. The average processing time for new business was 22 days; however, it could take as long as 45 days to approve or disapprove an application, especially if the applicant's prior driving record had to be obtained from another state. If the applicant so desired, the requested coverage began immediately even though final policy issuance must wait for underwriter approval.

In some cases, the applicant's prior driving record indicated much higher risk than the member had indicated upon filing his application. It was possible that these members would not receive final approval, and therefore, a portion of their initial premium was returned. However, any claims made against these drivers during the underwriting period had to be paid by the Club.

The underwriting group, housed at the Los Angeles Headquarters, was responsible for assessing risk associated with each application. Part of this assessment was a check of the Department of Motor Vehicle records to verify the accuracy of the member's application. Upon recommendation by underwriting, the paperwork was forwarded to the Costa Mesa Processing Center (CMPC), where it was coded and entered into the computer system.

At the Processing Center, approved applications were processed into policies, initial payments were credited, and a policy/statement was mailed to the member. Members whose applications were declined were notified and partial payments were refunded. In either case, the responsible district office was notified in the form of a "purge list" and then the district office paperwork was destroyed.

It was company policy that all paper files were to be stored and maintained at CMPC. A principal reason for centralizing the files was the cost savings associated with economies of scale. Until the mid-1970's a duplicate file was located in each district office. The duplicate file was replaced with computer terminals in each office, providing "on-line" access to policy information. However, the on-line system contained most, but not all of the information found in the paper file. Requests for information not available on-line had to be handled either by telephone or via the mail system. From time to time, the requested file would be unavailable for some reason (such as an internal audit), and a member's question would have to be deferred until a later time.

Insurance: A Paper Intensive Business

Insurance administration was a very paper intensive activity at the Club. Each active policy required a distinct folder which contained a large array of different forms and documents consisting of an initial application, policy changes, questionnaires, etc. Many of these paper documents were generated from the Auto Club's own computer; a file copy would be printed for the paper file whenever a form was sent to the policyholder. In addition to the massive amount of paper for the active files, legal requirements mandated that the files on all expired policies be kept for seven years after the policy had been terminated.

The volume of paperwork was staggering. In an article from Best's Review (February, 1990), an insurance industry publication, Tom McKernan described the processing area of the Auto Club as follows: "If the 110,000 linear feet of insurance files at the Automobile Club of Southern California were stacked in a row, they would stretch for 21 miles." It took well over 100 employees just to manage (not process) the flow of this paper, and the storage area for the active files alone (56,000 sq. ft.) compared to the size of several football fields. Insurance processing alone amounted to 33,000 pieces of paper per day.

The Auto Club had long recognized the need to find better ways to manage the record keeping associated with the insurance business, and had a successful track record in the use of technology to reduce costs and improve customer service. Paper files were eliminated from the district offices in the mid 1970's with the development of a computer system which allowed data retrieval (but not alteration) via terminal. In the early 1980's, a toll-free 800 number was installed for policyholders to call directly to the processing center where service representatives had both terminal and paper file access to the information required to answer a policyholder's question.

The massive and growing amount of paper continued to be a major factor in constraining ACSC's ability to reduce costs and increase customer service. It was not uncommon for a policyholder's paper file to be "temporarily misplaced" when a request for that file was received. The personnel and real estate needed to manage and store the paper files increased the cost of doing business, while the problems inherent in routing and storing the files, at times, degraded customer service in the form of delayed answers to customer inquiries.

The Technological Climate At ACSC

The Club had long been a user of technology as a means of improving customer service. Tabulating equipment had been used in the 1920's and 1930's, and the first computer, an IBM 650, was installed in 1956. There continued to be a strong and ongoing relationship between ACSC and IBM.

In the mid-1970's, district offices were equipped with CRT terminals and eventually all paper insurance files were centrally stored in the Costa Mesa Processing Center. Most computerized policyholder information could be accessed via terminal by the district office, non-computerized information contained in the paper file, such as notes and written requests, were no longer easily accessed by the district offices, which were now fileless.

A district agent would have to request (by phone or the Club mail system) a specific piece of information from the Processing Center and a file clerk would have to locate the paper file, find the specific document and then either relay the requested information by phone or copy the document and send it back to the district office by Club mail. More recently FAX was used to relay these documents. If a file was off the shelf (either misfiled or being used elsewhere in the Processing Center), a customer's request could take hours or sometimes days to answer.

This was clearly not considered to be good customer service. As Mary Magee, Group Manager, Processing Administration, pointed out: "Fast access gives the customer the sense that you care and that you know what you're doing. The longer you keep a customer or his agent on hold, the more they feel that you are incompetent."

Club management had an ongoing interest in finding a technology which would reduce and streamline the flow and storage of the enormous amounts of paper documents. In 1976, a Kodak microfilm system was investigated, but was determined to be inappropriate because the documents were stored sequentially based on the date they were processed, and therefore, clerks had to handle many different rolls of film in order to reassemble each policyholder's file. For individuals used to having all of the information in one physical location, this dispersed storage system was unacceptable.

In the mid-1980's, companies, such as FileNet and Wang, introduced minicomputer - based imaging systems, which the Club investigated as a solution to their paper-based problems. These systems were limited in the number of allowable users (usually under 100), and therefore, if used, could only handle specific functions within the Club, rather than provide an enterprise-wide solution to the paper problem. Knowing that it needed a mainframe-based system, the Club naturally looked to IBM for the solution, but the response from the local IBM branch was that IBM had not entered the imaging market.

In 1987, it was discovered that USAA, a property and casualty insurance firm based in Dallas, Texas, had also decided that a mainframe-based imaging system was critical to the management of its paper-intensive business. USAA had successfully piloted a small project with a FileNet system (minicomputer-based) and subsequently searched for a mainframe-based system which could accommodate its entire operation. It had also entered into a joint development effort with IBM; the focus of the project was to transform the insurance processing part of its business from paper files into image files.

Tom McKernan and his key managers (in Administrative Services and Data Processing) visited USAA in order to determine whether the Club's needs could be satisfied with a similar image solution. After seeing the IBM-USAA prototype and meeting with various USAA managers, Tom returned to California convinced that the Club's solution to its paper deluge lay with this IBM product, which was not yet commercially available. Tom then pressed the local IBM branch to include the Club in the next phase of IBM's image system development.

In early 1988, IBM decided to form a strategic alliance with a select group of firms who had large-scale imaging needs. It wanted companies who had strong, top-level commitment to this technology and it wanted "early successes" to be able to use them as a "cheerleading group" when it eventually brought its system to market. In the summer of 1988, shortly after the Club was invited to apply for entry into this alliance, two IBM corporate executives visited ACSC and interviewed Tom and other high ranking executives to ascertain the level of IS sophistication within the Club and also to determine if there was a strong, high-level commitment.

The similarities that existed between USAA's and ACSC's business processes, as well as the fact that Tom had both the Administrative Services and Data Processing Systems groups reporting to him, convinced IBM that the Club should be chosen as one of the participating companies. Over 100 major corporations applied for the fifteen openings, which was later reduced to nine participants. By January, 1989 the imaging project was underway at the Auto Club.

The first phase of the project focused on scanning auto policy documents into the image system after they had been processed. The purpose of Phase I was to enable the organization to become comfortable with the storage and retrieval capabilities of the system before actually beginning to process documents directly on the image system. It was treated as a large-scale pilot project, and as a precaution against error, the paper documents were kept after they had been scanned into the image system. Phase II, scheduled to begin in the third quarter of 1990, would convert documents to image before they were processed. A significant reduction in the amount of paper storage was predicted because the paper documents would be destroyed after the scanning process.

Describing the Club's long-term objectives for image processing and other information systems technologies, Tom McKernan wrote in an October, 1988 memo:

> Our goal with this and other technologies should be to move toward the concept of a customer information "file" that permits all information available regarding a member's activities to be accessible through one set of operations rather than having multiple and separate "files" which do not easily allow integration of data to form an entire view of the member's accounts and activities. In thinking of how to employ these technologies, the focus should be on customer service, high quality, lower error rates, improved cost performance and improved employee job satisfaction. It is not necessary to think only in terms of how it is done or handled today.

ICON - The Club's Imaging Product

A detailed description of ImagePlusTM, the IBM imaging product, can be found in Appendix I. The Auto Club named its imaging project ICON, which stands for Image Capture Optical Network.

Image processing converted and stored a paper or electronic document into an electronic object or picture. An object, residing on a piece of paper could be decomposed into an array of small dots, (pixels or pels). When scanned into a computer, these dots would be converted into a bit string. The viewing of the stored object on an image terminal was very similar to viewing a picture on TV, in that the pixels were scanned quickly across the screen, so that the individual dots appeared as a complete picture.

Objects required considerably more storage space than coded data (textual information entered via a keyboard). Typically, one page (8 1/2 x 11) of coded data required 5KB of memory, whereas the same size page stored as an image required 50KB of memory. With thousands of paper images to be stored, the Auto Club needed more storage capacity than magnetic media such as disks or tapes. Large image processing systems required high capacity optical storage disks as part of their storage capabilities. These disks, each storing approximately one billion bits, looked like record platters; therefore, the hardware which managed these disks were called "jukeboxes."

As of 1990, optical disk technology did not provide a mechanism for writing over any existing information, and therefore, the disks were referred to as WORMs (write once read many). The image processing system at The Club consisted of scanners for entering paper images into the computer, indexing terminals to attach a "tag" or file name to the image for proper identification, image terminals for viewing and modifying the electronic images, the computer (CPU) which provided the "brains" for the system, the magnetic and optical storage devices, and the appropriate software to manage the CPU (operating system) and to manage the image documents and files (application software). To accommodate both ImagePlusTM and a new database management system (DB2) on the same mainframe, ACSC upgraded to an IBM 3090 Model 200E.

The Club had over 3,500 data terminals installed throughout its facilities; its goal was to provide image terminals at Headquarters and in all the district offices and at Club headquarters. CLUBNET, the telecommunications network which tied the various offices of the Club together, would require increased bandwidth in order to transmit images throughout its dispersed facilities.

The Club viewed two aspects of the image processing system as especially important to its efforts to reduce costs and improve customer service. Electronic storage used far less real estate than paper storage. While the Club's paper files occupied well over 56,000 square feet, the magnetic and optical storage devices required less than 1,000 square feet. The reduction in space as well as in the number of file clerks would be significant. The second important aspect of the imaging system was that any image document could be simultaneously viewed by more than one employee. When a district agent wanted to view any part of his customer's file, he would simply access that document at his image terminal. Delays in answering customer questions due to misplaced files would no longer occur.

Management was confident that most of the long-time ACSC employees, who were accustomed to working with paper files would be able to adapt to the imaging system. Although all documents within a paper file were stored together (in the file folder), the various documents in the image file would be stored on many different optical platters and/or magnetic disks. When a particular file was selected at an image terminal, the file's "Table of Contents" appeared on the screen. The viewer could then request and view each file document (individually) at the image terminal. The perception was that all images were physically located in the same place. This "bringing together all parts of the file at the terminal" (made possible by the application software) was considered to be of psychological importance to people who were accustomed to having all paper documents stored together in one file folder.

Internal Versus External Information

While many of the Club's insurance files contained documents which were externally generated, and therefore, needed to be scanned into the image processing system, the paper files also included "file copies" of all computer-generated forms sent to the policyholder. It simply made no sense to produce a hard copy of these internal documents and then turn around and scan these documents as images back into the system. Release 1 of ImagePlusTM did not offer a coded data capability; it provided no mechanism for cross referencing computer-generated coded data into the image index of a particular electronic folder other than generating a hard copy (via a printer) of this information and then scanning it back into the image system.

C.L. Murray, Systems Group Manager of the Data Processing organization and ICON Project Manager, noted there were two important reasons why the Club's system had to provide a way for the coded data to be internally tied to the image system. First, many of the processed documents were internally generated (of the 33,000 transactions processed daily, 20,000 were internally generated (coded data); therefore, it would be very costly in both personnel and computer time to print out and then re-enter (via scanning) this information into the system. Second, an image document required at least ten times the storage of coded data; therefore, storing coded data as image would result in the need for even larger magnetic and optical storage capability.

ACSC had worked with Image Sciences Corporation of Dallas Texas, in the development of software that merged coded data with the Club's computer-generated forms on a Xerox laser printer. Each of the over 100 different Club forms were designed in-house on a Sun workstation and then uploaded to the mainframe. IBM chose not to develop a coded data solution internally, but funded (together with ACSC) the coded data development at Image Sciences. This solution saved print time, scan time, optical storage space, and most importantly, personnel time which would have been needed to collect and then scan all of these internally generated documents.

The application software created by Image Sciences Corp. allowed each Club generated (blank) form to be stored as an image. When a specific form was required (coded data linked to the proper blank form), the system would store the links between the coded data, blank form and the electronic file to which this document belonged. Although these documents didn't really exist as individually stored images, the person wanting to view the document could make no distinction between internally or externally scanned documents.

In order to view any document in a particular file, the user selected that document from the file index. If an externally generated document were requested, the system simply fetched that stored image (which had been previously scanned) and presented it to the image terminal. If an internally generated document were requested, the previously created software linkages brought the image of the blank form and the coded data to the terminal and overlayed the coded data onto the form. From the viewer's perspective, it appeared as if each document (whether internal or external) was a separate stored image.

Project Management

ACSC used a number of mechanisms to facilitate user involvement in the imaging project. Four committees were established to manage the various components of the imaging project. The Executive Committee was composed solely of executive and senior Auto Club managers, while the three other committees, a Management Committee, an Applications Subcommittee, and Platform Subcommittee, consisted of both Club and IBM employees.

The Club used IBM's Joint Application Development (JAD) methodology to define the requirements for the imaging system. One of the key requirements of this systems development methodology was to have an expert facilitator that could lead the group through a set of structured activities. This was the first time the Club had used JAD and an IBM expert in JAD was brought to the Club to direct the two JAD sessions.

The paper (file) environment was reviewed and the requirements for the image environment were defined. JAD1, held on September 11, 1989, was attended by 26 people; the JAD session leader, two JAD analysts, one insurance specialist, eleven participants and eleven observers. JAD2, held on November 13, 1989, was attended by 23 people; the JAD session leader, one JAD analyst, fifteen participants and six observers. Phase II requirements were defined at this session.

According to Group Manager Mary Magee, the active participation of the employees in the JAD sessions really made them feel a sense of ownership; they had helped design the new system. This participatory feeling led to much greater acceptance of the imaging system. The present way of doing business was carefully reviewed to determine what was essential to run the business and what could be discarded. As Mary explained: "The JAD sessions made us look at each piece of paper saved and ask: "Do we really need this document?" It was amazing for us to discover how many unnecessary pieces of paper we were filing!"

Future Issues at ACSC

The Club planned to complete the conversion of its insurance administration processes from paper to image before it applied the image technology to claims processing. There was also interest in using the technology to streamline many of the Club's functions, such as membership, travel, map-making, and license renewal.

Prior to beginning the imaging project, the Information Systems group had begun a major new development project, PRIME (Policy Rating Issuance Management Excellence), which would eventually allow policies to be generated directly from the district offices. This would require an expert system component to assist district agents with underwriting decisions. A major part of PRIME entailed migrating ACSC's existing computer files to a database (DB2) environment.

Unlike the imaging project, which was developed by IBM and therefore required only a few Club analysts and programmers, PRIME was a large-scale, internal development project, which required many of the Club's analysts and programmers. When the passage of Proposition 103 required many changes in the insurance business, most of the professional staff assigned to PRIME had to be diverted to implement the required changes in the Club's computerized insurance system.

Interestingly, a fully implemented PRIME would eliminate much of the paper that had to be processed, because district agents would enter all information electronically, perform most of the underwriting tasks and issue a printed policy for the customer on the spot. By pursuing both a paperless insurance system and image processing at the same time, were the two systems at cross purposes or was the Club hedging its bets? Tom McKernan felt there was a need for both technologies within the Club and had recently re-energized the PRIME project by directing C.L. Murray to make it a very high priority.

Improving ACSC's competitive position was senior management's top priority; the task was complicated by the many negative aspects (regulatory changes, assigned risk, litigious society) of the automobile insurance industry in Southern California.

Management recognized they needed to increase the number of Club members and also increase the percentage of members who bought automobile insurance through the interinsurance exchange. Although the Club was a major player in the motor club market, there was growing competition from a number of rivals, including Montgomery Ward, Allstate and Amoco.

To attract more of its members into the exchange, the Club needed to reduce costs, so that it could offer more competitive rates. ICON and PRIME could significantly reduce labor costs. However, employee loyalty was valued by the Club and it had a history of providing stable long-term employment. Senior management felt that the Club's employment record was good; as technology was introduced to the Club over the past forty years, new and usually better opportunities were found for those employees displaced by the technology.

Yet ICON and PRIME had the potential to have more far reaching effects than previous technological changes. Forty positions had been eliminated during the first year of the ICON project; this dilemma presented management with some difficult decisions ahead. Could the Club continue to use technology aggressively and still provide job security and upward mobility for all of its 5,600 employees?

EXERCISE

1.   Develop an analysis of the impact of changing governmental regulations on the work activities of ACSC.

2.   Develop a proposal to justify the alliance with IBM for this project. What are some of the risks involved?

3.   How can image processing technology improve the customer service activities of the Automobile Club of Southern California?

4.   What type of legal issues must be considered when hard copies of documents are no longer retained?

5.   What are the risks involved in storage on optical disks when no one is certain of the maximum life-span of such storage technologies?

APPENDIX I
Detailed Description of ImagePlusTM

ImagePlusTM is IBM's image processing solution for high-volume image processing needs in the Multiple Virtual Storage Enterprise Systems Architecture (MVS/ESA). The following description of ImagePlusTM is excerpted from IBM's MVS/ESATM ImagePlusTM General Information Manual.

The IBM MVS/ESA ImagePlus system is designed to replace warehouses full of file cabinets with a system of electronic images. Capable of connecting over a thousand users at local and remote settings, the ImagePlus system supports the daily capture, storage, retrieval, distribution and processing of tens of thousands of document images.

The IBM MVS/ESA ImagePlus systems includes all the software and hardware components needed to bring image processing into your production environment. The ImagePlus system adds applications and storage management software, optical disk storage subsystems, and workstations to your existing information system components such as line-of-business software and magnetic disk storage systems. Optical disk storage offers low-cost, permanent storage, with the added advantage of direct access to this online information.

The system is built around an image product design that establishes a standard image communications data format, data stream, and protocols to which IBM image offerings will conform. These standards are intended to accommodate advances in image processing technology, allowing greater flexibility and device independence. A single MVS/ESA ImagePlus system can support multiple optical storage controllers, each with its attached storage units. The system is also designed to support remote configurations. Additional workstations can be connected to the system. Concurrent access, the ability for several employees to view the same document simultaneously (as opposed to only one employee, at a time, viewing a single paper document) is a major advantage of this system.

The Components of the ImagePlus System

IBM's ImagePlus system is composed of five major components: Folder Application Facility (FAF); Object Distribution Manager (ODM); Object Access Method (OAM); Optical Storage Subsystems Products; and PS/2 ImagePlus workstations. A brief description of each follows.

The Folder Application Facility (FAF) is a front-end application which automates traditional systems of filing, retrieving, and processing documents. The Folder Management feature maintains information about each document identified to the ImagePlus system and it provides an indexing function for images. The user can create his own identification scheme for storing scanned documents in electronic file folders,and can subdivide the folders by using tabs. FAF also provides a Workflow Management feature that automatically assigns work to system users based on the document's processing requirement and priority, and tracks the status of work that is awaiting processing.

Work assignments are automatically made to users according to their work assignment profiles. These profiles are created by system managers and supervisors using special management tracking tools supplied by FAF. Supervisors can also use the management tracking tools to grant supervisory authority to another user, grant document routing capability to users, and view and manage various work queues.

The Object Distribution Manager (ODM) works as a file server for image objects. ODM receives new image objects from scanner-equipped user workstations and routes these objects to the ImagePlus system's online storage components. ODM also routes the images to the appropriate workstation for processing. Positioned at the functional center of the ImagePlus system, ODM coordinates the activities of the system's major components. When a new image has been captured, ODM receives the new object from a scanner-equipped workstation and sends the object to the Object Access Method (OAM) for online storage. In response to user requests, ODM retrieves the objects from the OAM and delivers them to the appropriate user workstation.

The Object Access Method (OAM) provides system-managed storage for image objects. OAM allows the user to set retention requirements for documents and then uses this information to store image objects in a storage hierarchy consisting of high-speed magnetic disk and high-capacity optical disk library and shelf storage. OAM automatically stores, retains, migrates, and deletes image objects according to user-defined document processing cycles.

OAM stores new and frequently accessed objects on high-performance magnetic direct access storage (DASD). OAM subsequently writes these objects to an optical disk library and tracks all magnetic and optical storage disks on the ImagePlus system, including all library and shelf optical disks. It directs the mounting and removal of these disks in response to user need and also directs the staging of image objects between magnetic and optical storage for enhanced response time.

The Optical Storage Subsystem Products provide the high storage capacity needed to support large-scale image processing. This high capacity is available in economical form through write-once-read-many (WORM) optical storage technology. The Optical

Storage Subsystem Products include an optical library capable of storing 128 billion bytes of information online; this is the equivalent of over 2,500,000 scanned page images at a typical size of 50 thousand bytes per page.

The PS/2 ImagePlus Workstations are used to scan, display, manipulate, and print image objects. The ImagePlus workstations can be configured with a variety of scanners and printers. Images are displayed on one of two large-screen, high-resolution monochrome displays designed for use in ImagePlus systems. The IBM Monochrome Display 8508 is a landscape-style display that presents a full page of image and a full screen of data side by side. The IBM Monochrome Display 8506 is a portrait-style display that presents a full page of image and is used together with a separate data display (3270).

CASE 3
BANK SERVICES, INC.[1]

Jon Holm, the 36 year old President and CEO of Bank Services, Inc. (BSI), was thinking about his days at the University of Alabama. Of all the graduate courses that he had taken to earn his MBA degree, the business policy course was his favorite. He remembered how much he had enjoyed the intellectual challenge of identifying problems and recommending solutions for the "case" companies. Ironically, he must now do the same thing at Bank Services, except that now the challenge is much more personal and the environment is very real-world. Even though this first day of October is still warm, he can't enjoy the day because of the decision which he has to make before October 29.

The events of September had been unsettling to Jon, yet he knew they were inevitable. BSI's parent company, Southern National Corporation (SNC), was suffering from a decline in earnings. Of the 18 subsidiaries under the SNC umbrella, only two were reporting significant profits by the end of the third quarter. One was Southern National Bank and the other was the Southern National Investment Group.

The other 16 subsidiaries were dragging down overall profit to such an extent that by September, the parent SNC was showing an operating loss. This led to the forced resignation of Hal Jackson, who had served as SNC's Chairman and CEO for the past eight years. The Board of Directors replaced him with Bruce Smith, who was President of Southern National Bank. By late September, Smith had, through aggressive management, abruptly closed several of the most unprofitable subsidiaries.

---

[1]   This case was written by J. Barry Gilmore, Memphis State University and Guy Moore, General Mills, Inc.

After completing these closings, Mr. Smith then asked to meet with Jon on September 28th.

The meeting was cordial and to the point. Mr. Smith realized that Bank Services was showing a small loss in this fiscal year, and that the subsidiary had been profitable in 1983. Even so, Mr. Smith wanted a plan of action for restoring profitability to Bank Services in the current year and a list of recommendations for continued operations in 1985. He asked Jon to complete his plan and report back to him on October 29th.

After briefly reflecting on his meeting with Mr. Smith and the events of the past month, Jon began to organize his thoughts about Bank Services.

History of Southern National Corporation

The company had received a state banking charter in 1874, under the name of Farmers Bank of Alabama. As the name implies, the bank positioned itself as a farmers' bank and followed this agricultural strategy for forty-five years. By 1919, the bank was the largest financial institution in the region and one of the largest in the South. The bank realized that the region's economic emphasis was shifting from agriculture to industry.

This changing economic emphasis caused the bank to adopt a more industrially oriented strategy for the future. Between 1920 and 1960, the bank concentrated on commercial and business lending, giving it the image of a merchant's bank. In 1930, a federal charter was obtained and the bank's name was changed to the Southern National Bank and Trust Company. By 1939, Southern National Bank and Trust Company ranked 86th among the nation's 100 largest banks in terms of deposits. The next twenty years was an era of high growth in which the population of Birmingham nearly doubled while the total assets of Southern National Bank more than quadrupled to almost $430 million.

During the 1940-60 period, Southern National Bank was gradually building its correspondent business, thus becoming a banker's bank. A correspondent bank is a larger bank which provides banking services to small banks and serves, in effect, as a "bank for banks". By 1960, more than 400 banks in the region maintained an active correspondent relationship with Southern National Bank, giving it a national ranking of 32nd among the largest banker's banks.

In 1961, after the bank automated data processing with its first computer, the correspondent business strengthened dramatically. By 1969, 100 years after organization, total assets exceeded $1.5 billion. With deregulation looming in the future, the bank organized itself in 1972, as a bank holding company named Southern National Corporation (SNC).

Deregulation of the Banking Industry

Deregulation was the ultimate driving force behind SNC's strategy to become a non-traditional bank. In the mid 1970's, the company had begun planning for deregulation, which began with the passage by the U. S. Congress of the 1980 Monetary Control Act and the 1982 Garn - St.Germain Act. These acts phased out the ceiling on rates paid to depositors and allowed banks to offer a range of products in competition with money-market funds. Deregulation essentially created a new and different environment for banks and savings and loan institutions services by allowing them to compete with non-bank institutions.

Deregulation in the financial services industry was brought about because of the increase in competition from non-traditional financial services organizations. These non-traditional organizations began offering financial services in direct competition with banks and savings and loan institutions. Firms such as Merrill Lynch, Sears, American Express and Prudential/Bache offered virtually every financial service that banks and saving and loans could provide. In addition, these firms also offered ancillary services which banks in 1980 could not legally provide. These services might include the full range of insurance and employment relocation services. These firms became known as "financial supermarkets" due to their wide range of services.

The Banking and Savings and Loan Industry complained bitterly about the inequality of legislation which allowed these "financial supermarkets" to compete in the marketplace with virtually no regulation. These "financial supermarkets" were not subject to the interest rate ceilings on deposits and loans to which banks and savings and loan institutions were forced to adhere. Congress was pressured to pass legislation which would allow banks and savings and loan institutions to compete more effectively in the marketplace with these "financial supermarkets."

Two major pieces of legislation passed by Congress in the early 1980's deregulated the banking and financial services industry. These two statutes were the Depository Institutions Deregulation and Monetary Control Act (DIDMCA) of 1980 and the Garn - St. Germain Depository Institutions Act of 1982. These acts were drafted in direct response to pressure to increase the degree of competition in the financial services industry. The major impact of DIDMCA was the lifting of the restrictions placed on depository institutions regarding the interest rates paid for deposits and loans.

The Garn - St. Germain Act lifted the restrictions which had been placed upon the type of services offered by banks and savings and loans. Deregulation increased the amount of completion in the marketplace by effectively allowing depository institutions to compete with the "financial supermarkets" without excessive regulation. This new non-bank competition and bank deregulation had severely curtailed a bank's traditional way of making a profit. Before deregulation, a bank paid a certain percentage for deposits taken in and then received a higher percentage on the same money by lending it out. The spread between these percentages represented interest income for the bank. After deregulation, the ceiling on interest rates paid to depositors was dropped as nonbank competition entered the market by paying higher interest rates for deposits, forcing banks to operate with much lower spreads and thus lower profits. With profits decreasing, SNC focused on new strategies to generate income.

By the early 1980's, SNC had begun making another strategic transition, with banking deregulation serving as the major impetus. In the past, strategies had focused on the traditional practices of depositing and lending money for customers, regardless of whether they were farmers, merchants, or correspondent banks. This new strategy focused on the concept of becoming a "non-traditional bank," with the emphasis on marketing financial services to provide fee-based income as opposed to interest-based income. Management believed this radical new strategy was called for because of the significant changes in the banking environment. In order to provide organizational direction as SNC moved toward non-traditional banking, a Statement of Business Development Policy (Exhibit l) was circulated among management and staff of SNC. By 1984, in response to the policy change, SNC owned 18 subsidiaries, most of which were operating as non-traditional banking businesses. Bank Services Inc. was one such business.

Bank Services, Inc. - The Information Company of SNC

SNC organized Bank Services, Inc. as a wholly owned subsidiary in November, 1982. The concept of Bank Services materialized as a result of several environmental factors:

1. During the mid 1970s, SNC became acutely aware of the cost efficiencies achievable through automation after implementing significantly newer and more advanced computer technology systems in the organization.

2. In the late 1970s, SNC had chosen to maintain close ties with its correspondent banks while many other large banks had abandoned the business of performing daily processing services for their correspondent banks.

3.   By the early 1980s, deregulation, which SNC had anticipated earlier, began substantially increasing the operational costs for banks and savings and loans. This necessitated the need for these institutions to automate and reduce costs, in any way possible while expanding service available to their customer base.

4.   As the mid 1980s approached, the advanced automation capabilities of SNC enabled the firm to deliver improved and expanded service to its customers at a lower cost than the competition.

Exhibit 1
EXCERPTS FROM THE STATEMENT OF BUSINESS DEVELOPMENT POLICY

...The mounting pressures on earnings throughout the banking industry are visible results of the general breakdown of traditional banking practices. Unfavorable trends in major indicators point to an end of banking as we know it within our current decade. Banks that cling to their traditional roles as gatherers and lenders of money will become unprofitable and their remnants will be absorbed by more contemporary organizations...

...However, banks able to restructure as conduits for money and providers of financial services on a fee or percentage basis, and that have the necessary capital strength and financial acumen, will prosper. In this new environment, banks will become primarily marketing organizations. Their success will be increasingly determined by the sales effectiveness of their officers and the ability of these individuals to locate, structure, and consummate profitable business opportunities...

...Southern National Bank will rank high among those banks that survive the coming shake-up of the banking industry. This is because we are prepared. Also, just as we have not hesitated in the past to face difficult decisions and make the immediate sacrifices needed to assure the Bank's stability, this strength of leadership will continue. Those who can adjust to the new realities of the marketplace will find the years ahead challenging and rewarding.

(Signed)
Hal Jackson, Chairman and CEO

(Signed)
Bruce Smith, President and CAO

Because of these environmental factors, SNC believed there was a significant opportunity in the market place for a subsidiary which could provide information processing services to smaller banks. Thus, on November 10, 1982, SNC transferred $3.5 million in net assets to Bank Services, Inc. (BSI) in exchange for shares of BSI's common stock. The transfer consisted of tangible assets and liabilities of the Data Processing Division of Southern National Bank. Also transferred was the ownership of all existing software systems and those under development, plus all applicable contracts with customers and vendors. One part of the assets transferred to Bank Services, Inc. was the Overnight System.

The Overnight System

The Overnight System was a custom combination of distributed data processing hardware, software, and services designed to meet a community bank's need for lower data processing costs as competition increased. It was believed that the Overnight System would reduce a client bank's daily data processing costs from 30% to 40%.

The data processing equipment at the client bank's location would maintain all of the client customer's account information. The community bank could access and retrieve information quickly and efficiently because the system and information was at their site. This on-line service was different from other "on-line" systems because there were no dedicated long distance lines to another computer. Overnight terminals were tied directly to the client bank's in-house hardware. This distributed capability using NCR brand computer equipment, allowed the client bank to maintain their database, gave them the computer capacity for processing other work they might choose, and provided a powerful customer linkage to Bank Services.

During the day, the client bank would set up new accounts, make name and address changes, place holds on accounts, and make customer inquiries, all on-line and instantly. At the end of the day, the bank would call Bank Services and the information would be automatically transmitted to the Bank Services' data processing center at the Birmingham headquarters. Bank Services would receive the data in the afternoon, process the work, and transmit a fresh database back to the client bank every morning. The client bank would then print their reports and their customers' bank statements.

Customer balances and other banking information would always be current and instantly available through the Overnight terminals. This remote data processing concept would allow the client banker to get a good nights sleep at the end of the day without worrying about data processing.

Because transmission of data occurred for only a brief period of time in the late afternoon and early morning and regular phone lines were used to transmit the data, the service was not geographically limited. Thus, a Bank Services' client bank could continue current check clearing arrangements with its existing correspondent bank in order to get the best availability of money. The Overnight System, because it was a remote bank data processing system, would not interfere with a client bank's correspondent relationship.

Once the Overnight System was operational in a community bank, the system required no programmers or software technicians at the site. When problems surfaced, Bank Services would activate its remote diagnostics service capability through a telephone modem. Therefore, Bank Services technicians located at the Birmingham headquarters could then perform software services equivalent to those performed on-site, including changing programs and recompiling software.

In order to use the Overnight System, the typical bank, one with assets totaling about $100 million, would incur an initial capital expenditure of approximately $125,000. This $125,000 investment would be recaptured over time through lower processing costs because the transaction processing charges of the Overnight System would be less than the technical staffing cost of an in-house system. A cost comparison of a smaller bank contracting to have an outside vendor perform this data processing function versus the costs associated with installing an Overnight System was performed. Typically, if the smaller bank choose to perform the data processing function internally their, cost could be from 50% to 75% higher than using an outside vendor. In addition, the Overnight System's processing charges represented the expertise of twenty-five full-time and fully-trained software specialists which are not be available to a small bank.

Expansion

Throughout 1983, Bank Services sales effort had been most successful in the states of Alabama, Tennessee, Georgia, and Mississippi. This geographic area had been Southern National Bank's major area of influence for over 110 years. However, BSI's management believed a broader geographic customer base was crucial because at the end of 1983 Bank Services was still obtaining 70% of its revenue from Southern National Corporation and its subsidiary banks. The other 30% was coming from banks that had a correspondent relationship with SNB.

Sales efforts during 1983 had been handled by the correspondent banking division of SNC and top officers of BSI. By early 1984, three account executives had been hired to sell the Overnight System. As of September, 1984, all systems sold had been sold to banks that were either SNC subsidiary banks or correspondent banks of Southern

National Bank. The account executives were finding strong sales resistance from non-correspondent banks in the marketplace.

To achieve the goal of penetration in a broader market, Bank Services' Management believed BSI would have to continue increasing its financial industry visibility and capitalize on successful Overnight System installations to launch into adjacent market areas. BSI would also have to continue working on its software to enhance the product and differentiate itself from the competition. The goal of Bank Services, Inc. was to have at least 150 Overnight Systems in place by 1987.

Exhibit 2
BSI STRATEGIES

Date: April 17, 1983
FROM: Jon Holm, President
TO: Executive Staff

SUBJECT: Strategies for BSI developed in March 19 meeting are outlined below:

1. Reinvest approximately 3.0% of the five year pro forma revenue in research, development and product enhancement,

2. Through high performance and extensive support develop consistently long-term relationships including being the survivor data processing company in customer mergers and acquisitions.

3. Boost company and product visibility through national advertising and participation in major industry events and major state events in populace, unit banking states.

4. Create alternate channels of sales/distribution.

5. Sell an Overnight franchise in selected states, to a medium sized regional bank, which has a strong influence in a particular geographic area.

6. Develop and employ a remote sales force in selected states.

7. Expand into the savings and loan industry.

This goal was to be accomplished through a series of strategies developed by Mr. Holm and his management staff in April, 1983. These strategies are shown in Exhibit 2. Management believed this expansion strategy would extend Bank Services' market-place into all or part of twelve southern states, Eastern Texas, Louisiana, Arkansas, Southeastern Missouri, Southern Illinois, Kentucky, Tennessee, South Carolina, Mississippi, Alabama, Georgia, and Northern Florida.

Bank Services had undertaken a very aggressive expansion strategy because, based on their pro forma profit figures, the Overnight System was very profitable. Due to the fixed cost/variable cost ratio inherent in the Overnight System, overall profit for Bank Services was expected to be a substantial contribution to Southern National Corporation's future profits.

The Bank Data Services Industry

The financial industry purchases an estimated $4.25 billion annually in data processing services. The breakdown of these purchases falls into the following four groups with in-house systems representing the largest at $2,100,000 expenditures annually. Batch (paper-based) systems represent $910,00 with Overnight System's market segment of remote (distributed) systems representing $825,000 annually. Facilities Management contracts represent $410,000 in annual expenditures.

The in-house, remote, and facilities management segments were growing each year, while batch systems were either being phased out or, at best, maintained at "non-growth" levels. Bank Services believed that most of the batch banks would logically convert to a remote system before progressing to an in-house system. It was also believed that a majority of financial institutions would lease or purchase their data processing resources from external vendors in ever-increasing numbers between 1983 and 1990.

In the United States, there are approximately 14,600 commercial banks. With the advent of high-speed data communication and data processing equipment, Bank Services believed its market was geographically unlimited. One limitation they did face was the number of banks of a certain size that could utilize the Overnight System.

Bank Services marketed the Overnight System to community banks with total assets between $50 and $300 million. Banks within this size range usually did not have the expertise nor the capital required to develop, manage, and maintain costly in-house information systems. Banks smaller than $50 million in total assets generally could not justify the cost of the Overnight System, opting instead to purchase a mini-computer system with packaged software. This left a significant gap in Bank Services' ability to service over 70% of the banks in the United States; namely, banks with

$1 to $50 million in assets. Since the Overnight System was too expensive for their needs, the Linchpin System was developed to allow Bank Services to meet the cost and service the needs of small banks with less than $50 million in assets.

Linchpin - Bank Services' Response to the Gap

Unlike the Overnight System, the Linchpin System was a stand-alone, in-house computer system that operated totally independent of Bank Services. Also, the Linchpin System utilized IBM hardware as opposed to the NCR equipment used by the Overnight System. The Linchpin System software was developed and licensed by Bank Services. The Linchpin System was fully developed and ready for the market by mid 1984. A typical Linchpin System sold for approximately $50,000 with gross margins expected to equal or exceed Overnight's margins. It was estimated the Linchpin System would cost the typical bank approximately $15,000 to $25,000 per year in operating costs.

Although the Linchpin System could handle the data processing needs of a $50 to $300 million bank, the System was targeted to the less than $50 million bank. These smaller banks accounted for over 70% of the banks in the United States and represented a major market for Bank Services. Overnight and Linchpin Systems in tandem gave Bank Services a product line that was capable of servicing 95% of the domestic banking market.

As a turnkey system, Linchpin had all the capabilities that the remote system offered. This product for the small bank was an important part of Bank Services' strategy. Bank Services believed that small-bank Linchpin sales today would be larger-bank Overnight sales tomorrow. As these smaller banks outgrow the Linchpin System, Bank Services expects the client bank to move from one product to another, that is, from the Linchpin System to the Overnight System. This migration was very important strategically to Bank Services in terms of continuing long-run customer relationships.

Competitive Environment

The data processing industry was highly competitive. Bank Services believed that the principal factors affecting industry competition were product availability and comprehensiveness, software flexibility and ease of use, software enhancements and maintenance, software adaptability and ease of change, customer support, training, documentation, customer relations, and references.

Bank Services competed with many other large banks who offered software products that were very competitive with the Linchpin and Overnight Systems. Among the big national banks that had data processing centers in various parts of the country were Citicorp (New York) and Bank of America (San Francisco). The largest national provider of data processing services among all banks was the Mellon Bank of Pittsburgh. Bank Services also competed directly with very powerful Southeastern regional banks such as Republic National Bank of Dallas, North Carolina National Bank and Citizen & Southern Bank of Atlanta. Appendix I provides brief sketches of some of these competitors.

Regional and local competition from medium-sized banks was particularly strong in some areas of the Bank Services' marketplace. The above mentioned banks usually competed very effectively in their "area of influence" because of their reputation and also because the regional bank's management have personal friendships with officers of these smaller banks. Bank Services was also faced with market resistance from present and potential client banks who may have chosen to develop their own custom application software and then subsequently market their own software and/or system.

In addition to banks, Bank Services competed with computer service companies that provided data processing services to the financial industry, including such giants as Control Data Corporation of Minneapolis, Electronic Data Services of Dallas, and Automatic Data Services of Atlanta. Bank Services believed that no one firm could be considered as dominant in providing application software or third party services to the banking industry. In addition to these industry giants, there were a number of regional service and/or software companies which had greater financial and management resources than Bank Services, and the technological ability to develop products similar to the Linchpin and Overnight Systems.

Major computer hardware manufacturers, such as Burroughs and NCR, had made significant competitive inroads in the financial industry with specialized banking software. To date, IBM had not been an important factor in the specialized applications software market for financial institutions. Although many banks have IBM equipment in use, the majority of the IBM hardware installed in the financial industry was driven by third-party software.

Bank Services believed it had several advantages over the computer service companies and computer hardware manufacturers when it came to developing bank software. The most important one was the ability to keep up with banking laws. In the world of bank deregulation, changes were inevitable and a bank's survival depended upon the speed and accuracy of responding to a changing environment. No one was more in tune with the regulatory aspects of banking than a bank-owned company. To insure that the products it sold were as up to date as possible, Bank Services employed the same software development staff for both its client and the parent Southern National Bank.

Product Development - A High Speed Chase

The data processing industry was characterized by rapid technological change which required a continuing high level of expenditures for the on-going enhancement of existing software and the development of new software products. Development of applications software packages for the financial industry was a long-term and continuing process. Technological advances in computer hardware and operating software, in the midst of industry deregulation, have required frequent system modifications. Such changes in the technology and legal environments industry had also resulted in more complex and comprehensive data processing needs.

Bank Services was committed to the continued enhancement of its existing software product, realizing that a failure to do so would result in rapid product obsolescence. During 1983, Bank Services had spent $1.2 million in design, development, installation, acquisition, and modification of the system. Thirty full-time equivalent employees worked on the development, enhancement, conversion, and maintenance of the software systems. These employees could be grouped as follows:

Function	Employees
Systems Development	11
Modifications/Enhancements	9
Installations	7
Operating Systems	3

Bank Services was also committed to maintaining state-of-the-art hardware systems that would represent the leading edge of technology. Thus, Bank Services always used the vendor's newest and most advanced hardware in servicing the client bank.

On the drawing boards was the Overnight II System scheduled to be delivered by September 1, 1985. The Overnight II product was being designed as a more powerful distributed processing system targeted for larger banks and franchised-bank "hub" operations. This project would be organized as a separate Bank Services division similar to the current Overnight and Linchpin Divisions.

Conclusion

Jon remembered that Bruce Smith, while still President of Southern National Bank, had given an interview to a national banking magazine, stating: "The sale of services for fees is our future, not taking deposits and lending money. We don't think there is any future in that." Another high official in SNC had recently made the statement that: "SNC is becoming more of a computer company that happens to own a bank instead of a bank that happens to own some computer operations."

Even so, Jon was very aware that SNC wanted profits quickly, and any change in strategy which would cause Bank Services to have even probable short-term losses would not be acceptable to the present management. He certainly didn't want his division closed. Thus the plan which had to be submitted to Mr. Smith by October 29 had to answer two questions. What is the problem? How can it be solved?

EXERCISE

1.   Over the history of Southern National Bank, what strategic changes has it had to make?

2.   What are the significant industry characteristics and trends facing the banking/financial services industry?

3.   Given BSI's strategy, resources, and the environment in which BSI competes, what will be their probability of success?

4.   What would you recommend to Mr. Holm?

Appendix I
BANK SERVICES INC.
SELECTED REGIONAL COMPETITORS

NCNB

This Charlotte, North Carolina, bank holding company is the largest in the southeast, with assets totaling $15.7 billion. Because of the reciprocal interstate banking laws in North Carolina, NCNB has 153 banking offices in Florida along with 215 such offices in North Carolina. NCNB has processing centers in four North Carolina cities, as well as four Florida cities, which provide automated services for its 571 correspondent banks.

CITIZENS AND SOUTHERN Georgia Corporation

With $7.4 billion in assets, Citizens and Southern (C&S) is the largest bank holding company in the state of Georgia. This Atlanta based corporation engages in traditional correspondent banking with many smaller client banks throughout Georgia, some of which includes data processing services.

First Atlanta Corporation

As Georgia's second largest bank holding company in terms of assets, at $6.4 billion, this corporation is another major participant in the southeast correspondent banking market. Like its neighboring counterpart, First Atlanta generally offers nothing more than the basic correspondent services in the marketplace.

First Tennessee National Corporation

This multi-bank holding company headquartered in Memphis, Tennessee, is the largest in the state with $4.6 billion in assets. It's Information Services Group provides data processing services to 109 correspondent banks. Through its First Express division, participating banks across the country are offered check clearing and data processing services from over 100 cities via the overnight delivery system of Federal Express, which is also based in Memphis.

Third National Corporation

Totaling $4.2 billion in assets, this Tennessee banking holding company is another major competitor in the region. The Nashville-based corporation maintains data processing relationships with more 450 correspondent banks in the south, and has data processing centers located in four Tennessee cities.

Central Bancshares of the South, Inc.

This Birmingham, Alabama, bank holding company is a $3.0 billion institution in terms of assets and is the third largest bank in the state. Regardless of its size and rank, this company's Central Computer Services, Inc. provides correspondent and data processing services to 473 smaller banks in nine southern states.

Deposit Guaranty Corporation

This is Mississippi's leading bank holding company with $2.5 billion assets. In spite of a fairly substantial base of correspondent clients, this corporation recently chose to phase out its data processing in their sector of the market.

Union Planters Corporation

Based in Memphis, Tennessee, this $2.0 billion bank holding company has banking offices throughout the state. Part of it's financial services include data processing activities. Their data processing arm provides batch computer processing for its affiliates and correspondent customer banks in a three-state area.

Hibernia Corporation

This $1.7 billion New Orleans bank holding company is ranked first in the nation for consistent earnings-per-share growth during the last 10 years. Its 22.8% compounded growth rate for the period between 1973-83 is well above the 15% average growth rate of the top ten banks in the South. Its data processing services department uses the latest IBM mainframes for networking a number of financial institutions in Louisiana and Mississippi.

Citizens Fidelity Corporation

Located in Louisville, Kentucky, this $2.7 billion bank holding company provides data processing services to correspondent banks in Kentucky, Tennessee, and Indiana. The bank purchased the assets of a data processing business located in Lexington, Kentucky, to enhance its computer processing service.

CASE 4
COMPUTER WORKSTATIONS[1]

Sales of computer workstations are growing faster than any other segment of the computer industry at a time when sales of mainframes and minicomputers are slowing down and personal computer sales have levelled off. According to S.C. Berstein and Company, sales of computer work-stations are expected to increase at a rate of about 59% over 1988 but are expected to increase only 15% in 1990. If unit prices continue to drop and additional software is made available, workstation sales could surge again in 1991. Sun Microsystems, Digital Equipment, and Hewlett Packard currently possess about 70% of the workstation market, with IBM and a number of smaller companies accounting for the rest.

In contrast to personal computers, workstations are characterized by 32 bit instead of 16 bit microprocessors, the use of the UNIX operating system instead of MS/DOS, more sophisticated software and graphics capabilities, larger storage capacities, faster processing speeds, and the ability to function effectively in a networking environment. On the other hand, personal computers are less expensive and more flexible in working with mainstream software packages. DOS based personal computers are easier to use than workstations and networking is an awkward add-on to the stand-alone personal computer. PCs are sold mainly through retail dealers while workstations are sold by manufacturers sales forces or specialized resellers. As workstation prices continue to decline, it is likely that some lower priced models will be sold through retail dealers.

---

[1]   This case was written by William C. House, University of Arkansas and Walter E. Greene, The University of Texas-Pan American. Published with the permission of the North American Case Research Association.

The principal users of workstations have been engineers and scientists. However, price reductions and technological improvements have broadened the appeal of workstations so that they are finding use in financial trading, desktop publishing, animation, mapping, and medical imaging applications. Northrop Aerospace used 800 workstations to design the Stealth bomber while the Federal Reserve Board has employed a network of Sun workstations to design treasury bill movements. In both cases, mainframe solutions to the processing problems involved would have been two to three times more expensive. Mainframe manufacturers, including DEC and IBM, are still pushing mainframe computers since the profit margins on mainframes average 60% compared to 40% on smaller computers.

Workstations are often more powerful than minicomputers and serve one user at a time whereas minicomputers often serve 10 to 25 users. Mainframe computers use dumb terminals and shared resources to perform preprogrammed tasks. Dumb terminals controlled by minicomputers or mainframes operate at lower costs than workstations or personal computers but total implementation costs may be higher. Personal computers provide ease of use, familiarity of operations, and inexpensive hardware platforms with stable operations. At a higher cost, workstations provide technical flexibility, increased processing power, higher resolution graphics, and possible elimination of network servers. Since workstations normally use the UNIX operating system, users can run multivendor and mulitasking systems while personal computer operating systems are still proprietary in nature.

Workstations can handle larger files, process data faster, and provide better graphics and networking capabilities. Workstations are also more likely to be compatible with a wide range of existing hardware configurations. However, software, peripheral, and training costs are typically higher for workstations while a larger amount of software is available for personal computers. In essence, the price/performance ratio is the biggest difference between personal computers and workstations. Aerospace and automotive companies have often found that the extra computing power possible with workstations is well worth the higher prices and lack of flexibility.

As Table 1 shows, workstation sales in dollars have increased from $1.2 billion in 1986 to $2.6 billion in 1987 and $4.1 billion in 1988. Estimated sales for 1989 are $6.4 billion and for 1990 are $9.0 billion. The U.S. Department of Commerce estimated that approximately 220,000 workstations were shipped in 1989.

There are only a small number of vendors in the workstation market, which has well established standards and typically uses the UNIX operating system. Three major vendors have gained 70% of the market (Sun, Hewlett Packard/Apollo, and Digital Equipment Corporation). Market penetration has been very limited so far, with only about 3% of the primary target population of engineers, scientists, and computer

Table 1
WORKSTATION SALES FOR YEARS 1986 TO 1990 (IN BILLION $)

YEAR	SHIPMENT VALUE
1990	9.0*
1989	6.4*
1988	4.1
1987	2.6
1986	1.2

*Estimate

Sources: U.S Industrial Outlook, 1990. International Data
Corporation, New York Times, April 23, 1989.

Table 2
UNIT SHIPMENTS OF WORKSTATIONS AND PERSONAL COMPUTERS
FOR YEARS 1989 TO 1991 (000'S OF UNITS)

	WORKSTATIONS	PERSONAL COMPUTERS
1991*	700	13,009
1990*	467	11,944
1989*	305	10,976
1988	192	9,960

COMPOUND ANNUAL GROWTH RATES 1988-1991	54%	9.0%

Source: Dataquest, Wall Street Journal, March 20, 1990.
   *Estimates

systems analysts currently using technical work stations. Sales are increasing as they begin to gain a price performance advantage. Workstations now cost less than $10,000 in many cases, and are two to three times more powerful than personal computers.

Sun, Hewlett Packard/Apollo, Digital Equipment have 70 to 80% of the market with Intergraph and Silicon Graphics possessing about 11% of the total market. IBM has only 2 to 3% of the market and companies in the other category have increased their market shares from 9.0 to 16.0%, primarily at the expense of Hewlett Packard and DEC.

Table 2 shows actual and estimated unit sales of workstations and personal computers for the years 1988, 1989, 1990, and 1991. The compound annual growth rate for workstations is expected to be about six times that of personal computers, although unit sales of personal computers should be about fifteen times that of workstations.

Sun Microsystems

The market leader, Sun Microsystems, has a tightly focused product line and is phasing out older models not compatible with the Sparcstation line. The Sparc workstation, introduced in April 1987 for a price of $9,000, processes data at 12.5 mips, has a Unix graphical interface, and an optional MS/DOS connections. Scott McNealy, chief executive officer of Sun, says workstations are displacing PCs in a number of Fortune 1000 companies. Sun expects to introduce a new version of its Sparcstation in midsummer 1990 which will cost about $5,000.

Sun's strategies include focusing on lower prices, well developed marketing programs, and third party software development. Sun has been offering three separate workstations based on the SPARC RISC chip, the Motorola 68030, and Intel's 386 microprocessors. From 1,400 to 1,600 applications are available for the Sun Sparcstation compared to approximately 1,000 for Hewlett Packard and DEC. The company is licensing its SPARC chip to third party clone companies with the desire of expanding the installed RISC computer base. The overall company goal is to deliver a complete processing solution, including graphics, input/output, software, and networking.

Sun has emphasized sales growth for the past several years. For the four year period ending in 1989, Sun's average annual growth was 260% with the average annual profit growth reaching 70%. Sun executives became convinced that since the large computer hardware companies would eventually enter the workstation market, the company should go all out to increase market share no matter what the cost. At one point, the organization added more than 300 employees and a new sales office each month. Engineers developed a steady stream of innovative, but not always practical, workstation prototypes and products, which were sold largely by word of mouth with virtually no formal sales promotion programs.

By the summer of 1989, the company was experiencing production bottlenecks as discounted sales of older products mushroomed. Large backlogs of sales orders were not being entered in the inventory control system and the company didn't know what products it needed to increase or decrease in production. In addition, several key executives left the company.

In the last quarter of 1989, Sun experienced a $20 million loss due to misjudging consumer demand and incurring parts shortages. However, it posted a $5 million profit in the first quarter of 1990. Sun is changing its approach to place more emphasis on profitability and less on growth. Sun President, Scott McNealy has tied executive pay to before tax return on investment. The company is also expanding customer service and hiring fewer employees.

Hewlett Packard

Hewlett Packard recently introduced its 2500 series workstation with a processing speed of 4 MIPS which will cost $4,000 and will compete with some high-end personal computers like the IBM PS/2 and MacIntosh III. Hewlett Packard has an additional problem arising from its merger with Apollo computer, necessitating the consolidation of two different computer architectures. An extensive amount of time, effort, and money may be required to completely implement the changeover.

Digital Equipment

Digital Equipment, during the period 1984 to 1988, focused on one computer design and a single set of software programs used on all computers in the DEC family. During this period, sales increased 200% and profits increased 400%. In early 1989, DEC introduced a RISC based work station which has 8 megabytes of memory, processes data at 14 MIPS, and costs about $20,000. First year sales were approximately 5,000 to 8,000 units. One of DEC's principal concerns was whether the new station would take sales away from its popular line of VAX minicomputers. In fact, DEC sales personnel still push the VAX line for multicomputer solutions instead of focusing on the new workstation line.

Since 1982, a number of customers have phrased out DEC minicomputers and shifted into Sun or Hewlett Packard/Apollo RISC based workstations. Recent surveys indicate about twice as many customers are planning to buy Sun workstations as plan to purchase DEC workstations. Sun also has about twice as many software applications for its workstations as does DEC. Digital Equipment is striving to bring the DEC computing environment down to the level of personal computer/workstation users. President Olsen believes there is a growing demand for affordable desktop configurations that deliver more power than stand-alone personal computers and small networks.

DEC has experienced slowing demand and income levels. 1990 revenues are expected to be about the same as 1989 revenues and earnings are expected to decline more than 50% for the second year in a row due to workstation start-up costs.

IBM Introduces New Workstation Line

IBM's efforts to introduce a new workstation really began in 1986 when R. Andrew Heller moved to Austin, Texas to take over a newly formed independent unit designed to develop hardware and software technology for workstations. This unit reported to William Lowe, head of IBM's entry system division. Creation of an independent business unit was a strategy which IBM had followed before to avoid the strangling effects of bureaucratic IBM channels on new products. Mr. Heller announced that his goal was to pack the power of an IBM mainframe into a desktop machine built around the UNIX operating systems. In this operation, he had the support of Jack Keuhler, a member of the executive committee and John E. Bertram, a leading IBM researcher until his death in 1986.

In December 1988, two important events occurred. Mr. Lowe resigned to take a position with Xerox corporation and Terry R. Lautenbach, Senior Vice President, decided to transfer Heller to a new position as part of a move to transform the project group into a new workstation division and to tie the design laboratory more closely to marketing activities. Company executives said the move was a natural one, since Heller excelled in supervising start-up ventures but not in managing large ongoing programs.

Now slightly more than 40 years old, Heller was a brilliant aggressive designer of mainframes and higher powered small computers. He dressed in open shirt and cowboy boots rather than the white button down shirts, solid ties, and dark suits which have served as an IBM emblem. He was often referred to as "the wild duck who refused to fly in formation" by his IBM colleagues. Not only his dress code, but his commitment to pure technical performance in an organization which has always stressed marketing efforts ultimately led to his downfall.

Unhappy with his new position as a technical consultant and IBM fellow, Heller left the company in April 1989. Some industry analysts expressed the opinion that the reorganization of the workstation effort could result in a less powerful workstation than Heller's to be offered at a higher price that could make it less competitive with the company's existing computer products. Nicholas Donofrio, the new head of the advanced workstation division, maintained that the new workstation product would make IBM much more competitive in that market.

In February 1990, IBM introduced its new line of RISC based computer workstations, ranging in price from $12,995 to $100,000. RISC or reduced instruction set computing chips are faster and more powerful than traditional CISC or complex instruction set chips. CISC systems do not execute instructions as quickly as RISC chips, but have more commands and accomplish more with each command. RISC systems offer greater performance at lower costs and can generate more detailed graphics than

CISC based chips. About one-third of the workstations sold in 1989 were RISC based.

The new IBM RISC chip can handle as many as five instructions per second compared to other manufacturers' equipment. In floating point operations, IBM computers may be as much as five times faster than the competitors' equipment. IBM has promised it will have as many as 1500 software applications available for use on its workstations by the end of 1990. Sales of DEC stations have been hampered, a year after DEC introduced its new workstation line, due primarily to the slow pace of software development.

IBM plans to target its system 6000 to appeal to engineers and scientists who represent traditional workstation users. A second priority is to broaden its base to include users who are looking for high powered networked computers. IBM has strong ties to the commercial market for multiuser systems and is well positioned to meet the requirements of federal government agencies, corporate MIS departments, and large, widely dispersed network systems. In its efforts to promote workstation sales, IBM faces a serious risk of undercutting sales of high end PS/2 computers using the OS/2 operating systems. The AS/400 has thousands of business applications written for it while the RS/6000 will have few at first. Small business firms have expressed the greatest interest in workstations while larger firms have been the most frequent buyers of the AS/400.

IBM has hit middle ground in pricing although its new machines have good price/performance. Dollarwise, IBM's models are geared toward the upper end of the workstation market. Some competitors' products start as low as $6,000 to $10,000. IBM expects to increase its market share from 2% to between 15 to 20% by 1992 or 1993. If these goals are met, IBM could be generating four to five billion dollars in revenues by 1993 which would help its sagging sales in mainframes and minicomputers.

IBM also faces a credibility problem, since its original RT line which was introduced in the 1970's, was underpowered and overpriced. It never obtained more than three per cent of the total market. In contrast to PC's, where popular applications will run on almost any machine without major modifications, workstation applications must often be "ported" or rewritten to run on specific manufacturer's equipment. Despite IBM's assurance of numerous applications in a few months time, considerable user skepticism exists. A sizeable number of applications are available for DEC, SUN, and H/P workstations already on the market. Many customers will have to be convinced that performance advantages of RISC systems are greater than the cost of scrapping existing software libraries.

To succeed in the technical service market will require sustained superior price/performance and an extensive set of engineering/scientific software. Sun, DEC, and Hewlett Packard are now firmly entrenched in the technical workstation market with competitive products and extensive software offerings. Sun, with its single product line and a mixed service and support record, may have the most to lose from IBM's entry into the workstation arena. Cheryl Verdoe, of Sun's marketing division, says that IBM's emergence as a workstation supplier will expand the total workstation market by legitimizing alternative computer architectures and attracting customers who previously avoided UNIX systems. Several of the current workstation suppliers say they are planning to use IBM's entry as a selling point for RISC and UNIX based systems.

Availability of software, pricing policies, and market credibility are factors likely to determine the success of the new RT 6000 line. To gain market share, IBM may have to sacrifice some profitability at a time when its earnings are declining. If price/performance ratios are improved and market share can be increased or maintained, companies like DEC, Hewlett-Packard, and IBM can focus their large sales and service organizations on the workstation markets to gain competitive advantage. These three companies are in the best position to exploit the high end of the workstation market while Sun Microsystems is in the best position to succeed at the lower end of the market.

Current Developments in Workstation Market

Workstation makers are expanding their offerings with the goal of penetrating the high end personal computer market. Sun has announced a stripped down version of the Sparcstation Plus which will cost about $5,000 compared to $9,000 for the original version. It will have a monochrome monitor, no disk drive, no add-in card capability, and will run only UNIX programs. It is designed to be part of a network. The Digital Equipment $5,950 workstation runs almost as fast as the SUN unit. Hewlett Packard's 2500 unit costs $3,995 and runs about 40% as fast as the new Sun machine. MIPS Computers and Hewlett Packard plan new additions that will be competitive with other suppliers' machines.

A survey sent to 65,000 DATAMATION subscribers indicates that customer shipments of workstations for 1989 were expected to increase by almost one third compared to a ten percent growth in personal computer shipments and a ten percent decline in minicomputer shipments. About one third of respondents see a higher need for workstations in the future and foresee RISC architectures becoming the dominant technology used in workstations. Important criteria for workstation selection include quality/reliability, compatibility, CPU performance, vendor reputation/financial strength, and price/cost of ownership.

Current trends suggest changes in the way information systems managers purchase personal computers and workstations. They are beginning to be more concerned with price than compatibility, often buying from two or three suppliers rather than one. Users are mentioning price more often than compatibility in current opinion surveys.

Toshiba has announced the first portable workstation based on Sun's Sparc chip to be available in Japan by mid July 1990. With scientists and engineers being the major user of workstations, no clear indication exists of any sizeable demand for laptop portable workstation units. Toshiba's unit is 17.7 pounds (one-third the weight of Sun's workstation), has a fold-up screen, and runs at 13.2 MIPS. It is expected to sell for 2 million yen or $12,600. Forecasted sales are 14,000 units in 1990. It will be at least two years before a color monitor is available. The Toshiba machine is not battery powered or network oriented and must be plugged in to be operational.

Toshiba has been selling Sun workstations in Japan since 1986. Sony is the current leader in Japan with its NEWS workstation which was introduced in 1987. Japanese companies accounted for only slightly more than 15% of total worldwide workstation sales of $4.3 billion in 1989 but should increase their share of worldwide sales in 1990. The Japanese companies have lacked a complete line of software and distribution channels which would allow them to compete successfully with faster, RISC based US models.

Sony has announced a workstation based on MIPS RISC technology and may abandon the mainstream market to concentrate on a specific niche which would allow it to concentrate on its strong position in multi-media applications using Video and HDTV. Hitachi is planning to develop workstations based on a faster version of Hewlett Packard's RISC processor and Matsushita owns 52% of a Sun clonemaker, Solburne Computer. Cannon has invested 100 million in Steve Job's Next company.

EXERCISE

1. Develop a statement of product characteristics which would allow a workstation producer to differentiate its products from personal computers and minicomputers for use in advertising and promotion efforts.

2. Assess the growth prospects for RISC and CISC based computers, identifying situations in which each could be used.

3. In the face of increased competition, should SUN emphasize its higher priced or lower priced workstation line? Should Sun Microsystems target its lower priced workstations against high end personal computers, promoting and selling through retailers in a manner similar to personal computer makers? Why or why not?

4.   What target markets and promotion and distribution strategies should IBM pursue in order to improve its competitive position in workstation markets? What problems must be overcome to successfully pursue its strategies?

CASE 5
COUNTY AMBULANCE SYSTEM[1]

A county in Texas with a population of about 100,000 people is considering whether to continue its ambulance service or to hire a private company to provide this service. Since the 1950's the company has maintained one or more ambulances, usually stationed at or near the main hospital. In recent years the number of ambulances has increased to include four vehicles, outfitted with up-to-date medical support equipment. There is also a medical evacuation helicopter available as needed and located 100 miles away, for use in quickly moving patients who need special attention that is not available locally. Because the helicopter service is quite expensive and limited, most people prefer to use the ambulance service.

There are considerable differences in the functions, support facilities and costs associated with this county-wide ambulance service. The ambulance system includes special two-way radio coordination with various fire, police, and civil defense organizations in case of mass emergency; coordination with emergency medical and other technical professionals located in three different hospitals; and training and personnel development systems for attendants.

Calls typically come into the police department, and the police station dispatcher alerts the ambulance service by telephone. In some cases, police officers assist in moving the patient. The ambulance service also has a full-time dispatcher who serves as foreman for the various ambulance teams. The dispatcher maintains contact with ambulance drivers and attendants while they are enroute to calls.

---

[1]   This case was written by August W. Smith, President, Development Dynamics, a management consulting firm in Austin, Texas.

Administrative Systems

In addition, there are various administrative and paperwork requirements. The dispatcher must record each patient's name or description, time and date of call, location of accident or pickup point, age, address, telephone number, and nearest relative on a standard form. Often it is not possible to get this information directly from the patient, and some reported information later turns out to be incorrect or incomplete.

Often information is gathered under duress. In some cases, there is even conflicting information from several sources, each requesting an ambulance and unaware that someone else has already called in. Because no one is required to sign for the service at the scene of the accident, some patients later refuse to pay, contending that they did not directly request or contract for such service. Many have been unconscious and unaware that such service was ever rendered. There is a standard form for attendants to report all ambulance trips, times, and distances, along with a statement about the patient's condition at the time of pickup and time of delivery at the hospital or elsewhere.

In evaluating this ambulance system, it is important to consider the sources of information, when patients enter the system, how they are processed and how they exit the system. Also, the value or utility of this service to each patient receiver and how best to obtain feedback about the quality of services that were performed should be considered. This information is needed to protect the ambulance service from possible litigation and negligence suits, and to ensure that the service remains effective and efficient.

Since there is no other real competition in the area, service attendants could become complacent and the process become bureaucratic without standards of comparison. If problems should occur, it is important to evaluate performance and productivity of the ambulance service in all functional areas for which it has direct jurisdiction and responsibility.

At the scene of an accident, responsibility usually transfers from the police officer to the attendants once the patient is aboard the ambulance. Responsibility is then transferred to the hospital once the patient is admitted. Although this method seems simple, it is usually during the transfer of responsibilities that many problems arise. Each situation tends to be unique and requires judgements by the persons involved, often without the benefit of expert medical advice.

In 1989 the ambulance service received about 1,080 calls, and in 1990 there were 1,240 calls. About half of the calls entailed routine transfers of patients to hospitals within a five-mile radius of the major city in the area. The remaining calls involved special situations or transfers from outside the main area. These calls averaged about nine miles from pickup to delivery to the nearest or specified hospital. Since increased economic development started about 1989, the demand for service has grown substantially and is likely to double over the next five years.

With increased demand, it may be possible to add improved life-support and other special equipment aboard ambulances to provide additional services and meet more patient needs enroute to the hospital. Such improvements will mean increased expenses, however, and bad debts currently account for about 50 percent of monthly billings. Thus either charges to patients must be increased substantially or the county must underwrite a greater portion of the cost of providing ambulance service. Some community organizations have indicated a desire to help in limited ways to alleviate some of the immediate problems, but a longer-range solution is needed.

EXERCISE

1.   As an area system analyst, you have been asked to examine the current operations of this ambulance service and to make specific recommendations for improvements, including the identification of criteria or standards for immediate evaluations. What are the sources, inputs, processes, outputs, receivers, feedback channels, and environmental constraints on the operating ambulance system?

2.   What are the scope/jurisdiction and limitations of each component system involved in the overall ambulance system?

3.   What are the key objective output measures involved for each component system?

4.   List your recommendations and the standards you consider relevant to evaluating overall efficiency and effectiveness of the ambulance system now and in the future.

CASE 6
END-USER COMPUTING[1]

End-user computing encompasses development, implementation, maintenance, and use of information systems by individuals outside the information systems (IS) department. Its emergence and rapid growth during the 1980s has attracted the attention of both business professionals and academics.

End-user computing, however, exposes organizations to serious risks. User reluctance to test, document, and validate user-developed systems and the tendency to omit audit trails and operating controls increase the risks of end-user computing. The growth of end-user computing has also attracted management's attention with many agreeing on the need for some form of centralized planning and control. In many instances, these are provided by the information center, often controlled by and as a part of the IS department.

Some practitioners and academics, however, propose to manage end-user computing differently and even predict the demise of the information systems department in all but the largest business organizations. Users may create pressure for an environment characterized by complete user control over individual information systems, software selection, and data management.

---

[1] Adapted from "Evidence to Support the Continuing Role of the Information Systems Department in Organizations," Journal of Management Information Systems, Fall 1989, Vol. 6, No. 2, pp. 22-31, by Marius A. Janson, University of Missouri, St. Louis. Reprinted by permission of M. E. Sharpe, Inc., Armonk, NY 10504.

The Issue: Who Should Control Information Systems?

The relationship between the IS department and the end-users is an important managerial concern. It continues to be a subject of discussion that often results in contradictory advice and will have an impact on nearly everyone who works in the organizations of tomorrow. The following minicases contribute to this discussion by describing very different situations to consider from the perspective of "Who should control information systems?" The first minicase describes a highly competitive business environment requiring close communication between separate organizations. The second minicase, a computerized automobile dispatching system, concerns the implementation of off-the-shelf software. The third minicase describes off-the-shelf software for energy conservation that failed despite its modest complexity. These minicases show situations that give rise to complex problems not answered in terms of absolutes but call for more adaptive approaches to resolving problems.

Minicase 1: An Interorganizational System

Certain lines of insurance such as personal property, health, and travel, involve large numbers of customers who each take out relatively small dollar amounts of coverage. Processing insurance claims requires a great deal of information, usually supplied in written form by the insured party, which is then manually entered into the company's database. Often information on a single claim comes from multiple sources as a car accident may involve claims for auto repair, hospitalization, and personal liability.

Filing claims is frequently complicated because many insurance accounts originate at independent insurance agents. Much of this information is transferred by public mail, which is slow and is becoming increasingly more expensive. Reducing the paperwork flow between the insurance company, its customers, and its independent agents is an important cost-cutting strategy for the insurance firm: it simplifies the reporting tasks for the independent agents and customers, and it provides the customer with a speedier claims settlement.

Because of these advantages, linking independent agents to the insurance company's information system support functions will induce independent insurance agents to favor that company when signing up new customers for insurance. This benefits the company because it obtains a strategic advantage over its competitors.

With this in mind the Finnish insurance firm SAMPO started a pilot project to link its mainframe-based information system with the PC-based information systems of car dealers and trucking firms. The car dealers provided insurance to new car buyers, and the trucking firms purchased insurance for their trucking fleets. The software required in these interorganizational information systems was designed by the insurance firm with the cooperation of, but at no cost to, the participating organizations.

This business operates in a highly competitive environment and its information system is considered to be essential to achieving its corporate goals. Management would be averse to buying off-the-shelf software if this software would negate the company's advantage over its competitors. Furthermore, the application requires the exchange of large quantities of data between the insurance company's information system and the information systems of its independent agents.

Minicase 2: A System for Computer-Assisted Dispatching

A police car dispatching sequence typically begins with a call from a citizen for police assistance. The call is answered by a complaint evaluator who selects one of four courses of action:

(1) no need exists for a police response (e.g., caller requests the local town hall's address),

(2) no need exists for a police response, but a police report is required (e.g., caller reports his car stolen),

(3) a police response and a police report are required (e.g., crime is in progress), and

(4) a police response but no police report is required (e.g., police involvement is limited to directing traffic in an emergency situation).

Only in the last two situations is a police car required and the complaint evaluator places the request for assistance in a queue, where it awaits processing by the next available dispatcher.

Computer-assisted car dispatching (CAD) systems have been operating successfully for nearly 20 years. Thus, when the St. Louis Police Department required such a system, it was natural to look for standard off-the-shelf software that could operate on the department's mainframe. However, police departments differ in how they perform this day-to-day task. Additionally, police information systems, rather than being isolated entities, communicate and exchange data with regional and national information systems.

With these issues in mind, the department's database administrator, accompanied by several members of the police force, visited four cities with CAD systems similar in specifications to those needed in St. Louis. They selected a system in use in Kansas City because it used dispatching procedures in close agreement with those followed by St. Louis dispatching personnel. The only obstacles to implementing an exact duplicate of the Kansas City system in St. Louis were the dissimilar database systems of the two applications. The database administrator planned to bridge these differences by a partial rewrite of the software, which was not thought to affect the success of system implementation.

To ensure a smooth implementation, police personnel initially operated the modified system at approximately 20% of its intended capacity alongside the existing manual dispatching system. The entire cycle of dispatching a car requires information displayed on four different screens. In the modified system the dispatcher had to look at two screens at a time; thus, the completion of a dispatching task required alternating between screens. The time needed to alternate between screens was only a few seconds, but the St. Louis dispatchers considered this time to be much too long because it had the potential of placing police officers in undue jeopardy during crisis situations. Displaying all four screens simultaneously on one video display terminal, however, required significant changes in hardware and software.

Minicase 3: An Information System for Energy Conservation

Adequate information about energy consumption by end-use type is crucial in any effective energy conservation program. This case relates the failure of an energy information system installed to support the energy conservation effort for a midwestern state's publicly owned buildings. The energy agency purchased standard off-the-shelf software that had already been extensively used in other states to target buildings for energy consumption measures. The software was part of a system consisting of data collection forms, system operating manuals, and instruction manuals for staff members at individual buildings to help them complete the self-administered data collection forms. The agency collected data on approximately 300 variables for several thousand buildings and prepared reports indicating whether energy conservation measures were desirable. Subsequent analysis of these results by agency personnel revealed that the recommendations contained in the reports were erroneous and the system was abandoned.

This application seems a fitting candidate for commercial software because demand for similar information existed at other state energy agencies. Thus the availability of standard off-the-shelf software was likely, and no data exchange with other systems was required. Then what were the causes of its failure?

First, the energy agency was unaware that its objectives differed from those of the software house. The software house wanted a database for its own future use that contained as much information as possible on the energy consumption of publicly owned buildings. Thus, the amount of data collected was far in excess of what was needed for the energy agency's limited goal of targeting buildings for energy conservation measures. The data collection and data entry processes became unnecessarily complex and were sources of many data errors. The resulting poor quality data demonstrates that end-user computing without adequate attention to data integrity can place an organization at considerable risk.

Second, the software contained an engineering model for identifying buildings that consumed excessive amounts of energy compared to buildings with similar structural and operational characteristics. Because the model was incorrectly calibrated for climatic conditions and building characteristics unlike those found in the midwestern state, grossly inaccurate predictions resulted. The problems with the model and the data were uncovered after an in-depth study that required expertise on energy conservation, information technology, and statistical techniques for improving data quality.

EXERCISE

1.   Discuss the possibility of making the end-users the locus of control and responsibility for development and ongoing management of the insurance company information system discussed in Minicase 1. Would this be a reasonable approach to take? Why or why not? What role does this information system play in the strategic positioning of SAMPO vis-a-vis its competition?

2.   Minicase 2 discusses off-the-shelf software for police car dispatching. Would it be reasonable to put end-users in charge of the modifications to this particular system? Why or why not?

3.   Discuss the dilemmas inherent in acquisition of off-the-shelf-software. What are some of the advantages and disadvantages of such an approach to systems development. Use illustrations from both Minicase 2 and Minicase 3.

4.   What were the real problems that surfaced in Minicase 3? How could these be prevented and how does this relate to end-user management of the information systems effort?

CASE 7
ENGINEERS UNLIMITED[1]

The four telex rooms at ENGINEERS UNLIMITED were staffed by low level, clerical employees whose international messaging function was unquestionably very important to the company. Telex often provided the only reliable communications link into remote areas of the world where ENGINEERS frequently contracted to oil refineries or petrochemical plants. The introduction of a new and very different technology into the telex handling environment potentially influenced the effectiveness of ENGINEERS' main conduit for international business communications.

ENGINEERS maintained telex rooms in London, Atlanta, Trenton (NJ), and Philadelphia with each telex room utilizing paper tape teletype terminals. Typically, a telex message would be transmitted by a telex operator after establishing a direct-dialed telephone link between two such terminals. This process was slow and subject to frequent, and potentially costly, human and mechanical errors.

The new technology was a minicomputer switch with "store and forward" message handling software that allowed messages to be originated in the United States and transmitted over ENGINEERS' private data communications network to the switch in London. The switch would receive and store the message and automatically dial the destination for the telex through the public international telex network. The message would be transmitted without human intervention to its destination (almost always in the Middle East where ENGINEERS' major customers were located).

[1] This case was written by Charlene A. Dykman, University of Houston-Downtown.

Likewise, messages could be transmitted over the public telex network from the sites in the Middle East or other construction areas directly to the switch in London. The switch would then relay the messages to final destinations in the United States (often to ENGINEERS' offices in Atlanta, Trenton, or Philadelphia) over the private ENGINEERS' computer network.

Because of the differences in telex rates between the United States and the United Kingdom, the telex message switching architecture was highly cost effective. In addition, the switch automated many previously manual processes providing features such as automatic redialing of messages to sites where a "busy signal" was encountered, collection of traffic statistics for management reporting and for billing or cost allocation purposes, and abbreviation of frequently called numbers utilizing user-defined routing codes.

However, the primary savings opportunities were due to the differential telex rate structures between London and the US sites. Actual costs to ENGINEERS UNLIMITED for all message traffic traversing the system and being relayed through the London switch consisted only of the costs incurred to send messages to and from London and the job sites. This was because ENGINEERS' computer network was already in place, and there were no significant incremental costs in the network associated with this messaging system. The cost of the switch was minimal and insignificant in the overall economics of the project. Therefore, messages sent over the system often cost 10% less than the same messages sent from the United States to the same Middle Eastern destination.

The telex switching minicomputer was selected by a technical member of the corporate staff and installed in London with the expectation that telex room personnel would immediately adopt this means of sending telex messages. It was assumed that immediate and significant cost savings would be realized as messages from the United States would be sent over already leased computer network lines to London and sent at vastly reduced rates to their destinations.

Unfortunately, the implementation was a failure. Telex personnel refused to use the system for "important" messages. They did not trust the system. Instead they continued to use the old and familiar process with the higher costs involved. Several attempts were made to cajole, persuade, and even force the use of the system. After two years, the failure was recognized as a failure and a new team was brought in to analyze the situation and recommend a cost-effective solution.

Analysis of the Workflow

Under the original system of handling telex message traffic, each of the four main ENGINEERS UNLIMITED telex rooms functioned independently of one another and coordination of message traffic was minimal. The primary thrust of all such communications was with remote job sites, international suppliers of equipment and materials, and foreign partners. Essentially, they represented four similar but separate communications messaging systems. The impact of the switch implementation was to force these four separate systems to merge into one larger and much more complex system. This had a profound impact on the social subsystem of telex supervisors and operators who were expected to use the new system.

Before switch implementation, telex room activity could be described as clerical and highly routinized with workers organizationally isolated from other work groups. The only contact with other workers in the company took place when a hand-written or typed message was delivered to the input window of the telex room by the mail clerk or secretary of one of the functional departments. These messages were routinely keyed into the telex machine and sent to their various destinations.

The implementation of a system utilizing computer-based message switching technology fundamentally changed the nature of work in ENGINEERS UNLIMITED telex rooms. The telex rooms no longer formed mostly isolated, independent work groups. For example, the coordination of work efforts among London and US telex operators became critical. Telex personnel had to learn to interface with a much more complex technology to send and to receive telex messages. The London telex supervisor became a de facto computer system manager with all the complexities that are implied.

This system implementation represented more than just an enhancement of the telex handling process and mandated that the telex organization adapt in order to effectively utilize the new technology. There was no consideration of this interface between the social subsystem and the technical subsystem for this application as the implementation precipitated a major redesign of the individual jobs of the employees in the telex rooms throughout the corporation.

The telex switching system design had placed the entire focus on trying to make the best technical decisions in the selection of the minicomputer and associated software. Documentation of the effort existed in the form of memoranda, proposals, correspondence, etc. This documentation clearly showed sound analysis of financial data, hardware and software viability, etc. There was no mention of humanistic, behavioral, or organizational issues.

EXERCISE

1. What are the key subsystems that are involved in this case? How do these subsystems relate to each other? Diagram this relationship.

2. What do you feel are the real problems at the root of this failed implementation?

3. What was the scope of the original project? What would you recommend as the scope for a second attempt at automation of this process?

4. Develop a list of steps that you would recommend to address this situation.

5. Why would the tasks described in your list of steps contribute to a more successful systems implementation?

CASE 8
GUEST HISTORIES[1]

Service excellence will be the key factor in the success of hotels in the 1990s. One facet of service excellence involves remembering frequent guests' needs and desires, so that the hotel can fulfill those needs before the guest even asks. Consider the following hypothetical scenario:

Business traveler Chris Talioferro has just picked up luggage at the airport baggage claim. As Chris steps out to the ground transportation stop, the hotel courtesy van is waiting to meet the flight. In the van is Talioferro's favorite caffeine-free soft drink. Arriving at the front desk, the clerk greets Chris by name and asks for a quick signature on the hotel's registration card. All relevant guest information is already on the card, including the method of payment. Just to be sure Talioferro hasn't changed plans, the clerk confirms that payment will be by gold card. Chris can see that the assigned room is the same as during the last time at this hotel. During that visit Chris mentioned that its glass-topped dinette-style table was useful. Entering the room, the bellhop turns the television to the recently merged Disney-CNN network, which the housekeeper noticed was always on when Talioferro occupied the room before. In the closet are much-needed extra hangers, plus a personally monogrammed robe. On the table is the International Herald Tribune, the newspaper Chris requested during the last visit.

---

[1]   Adapted from Chekitan S. Dev and Bernard D. Ellis, Cornell University, "Guest Histories: An Untapped Resource," The Cornell H.R.A. Quarterly, August, 1991, pp. 29-37. Used by permission. All rights reserved.

67

Opening the mini-bar, Talioferro finds plenty of macadamia nuts (the mini-bar attendant noticed that five packages disappeared during Chris' last stay) and Famous Amos chocolate chip cookies. Chris also notices a bottle of Chateau Latour-1964, a preferred wine. Finally, Chris notes a message from the concierge telling about tickets to tonight's performance at the theater.

All of the services and amenities provided for the guest in this scenario are made possible by an automated guest-history program that was triggered when the guest's travel agent booked the room. Such individualized personal attention may be an important competitive strategy for hotels in the years to come.

Holiday and Hyatt Build Relationships

Holiday Inns has combined business and pleasure for members of its "Priority Club'" a frequent guest program. According to The Successful Hotel Marketer (January 7, 1991), Holiday Inn invited several hundred club members to complimentary getaway weekends, replete with theme parties and such speakers as Chuck Yeager and John Naisbitt. During the events, Holiday's marketers were on the scene personally asking the guests for their opinions on the Priority Club, Holiday Inn and proposed new concepts for the club. The chain also asked the guests about their leisure travel habits.

Hyatt Hotels and Resorts has created a recognition program for guests of its 22 resorts in the U.S., Mexico, and the Caribbean. Known as "Hyatt Gold Passport at Leisure," the program offers a special toll-free reservations number, priority reservations, and such special considerations during guests' resort stays as a manager's reception, a special concierge, and priority reservations and seating at restaurants. The "At Leisure" program is part of the Hyatt Gold Passport, which is the company's frequent-stay program for individual leisure travelers.

"Greetings" from Four Seasons

Four Seasons Hotels and Resorts began developing its guest history system five years ago, in an effort to improve guest service. The "Greetings" system is a proprietary software package designed to capture more information about customers than was possible with simple property-management systems. "Greetings" expands each individual hotel's PMS by allowing room for a more complete guest profile. More special-request codes are available and the system has plenty of open data fields to allow employees to enter guest preferences that do not have codes. If a frequent guest has mentioned a dislike for calls after 9 P.M., the hotel arranges to intercept late calls on all subsequent visits. Keeping track of that kind of guest desire was not possible with the PMS alone.

"Greetings" runs on a PC platform with an 80386 processor, and it requires substantial human supervision to maintain its effectiveness. A programmer at Four Seasons headquarters works full-time to enhance the system, while an operations system analyst ensures that the system's operation is smoothly integrated into daily operations. Support for each of Four Seasons' 27 hotels comes with a "Greetings" coordinator, who is responsible for keeping data complete and up to date. Most coordinators are recruited from the reservations department, which has long been responsible for noting guest requests. Management instructions and employee notes about special-guest treatment are given to the coordinator, who then determines which notes should be entered into the system. The coordinator is also responsible for merging guests' duplicate records. The result of this effort is a clean, accurate guest information data base that was generally unattainable with earlier guest-history systems.

Despite the cost in extra personnel, Four Seasons believes that the system has been a good investment. The company was pleasantly surprised to find that it had more frequent guests than it thought - 50%, on average - and these customers have given considerable positive reaction to the system.

In addition to accommodating guest requests, the extensive information captured by "Greetings" has added to marketing efforts by allowing marketing personnel to generate statistics based on any dimension of guest information. As a result, Four Seasons has a clear picture of where its customers come from and what their stay patterns are. Ad campaigns and direct mail have become more targeted, so that media dollars can be spent more effectively.

The development of "Greetings" has not been totally without problems. The interface with the property-management system is often awkward. Housekeepers now have their own "Greetings" terminal, and they have become directly responsible for finding guest requests that apply to them. That approach has lightened the load of the front office, whose employees commonly bear the full weight of guest requests. In implementing the "Greetings" system, Four Seasons also had to overcome a certain level of reluctance on the part of long-standing employees, who suddenly were asked their opinions on guest preferences. Universal access to the data base has caused some duplication of effort in accommodating known preferences. Four Seasons has concluded, however, that the last two problems are happy outcomes; namely, guests who are taken care of too well and employees who know that their input counts.

Four Seasons plans to enhance and expand "Greetings," notably by joining its individual hotel systems into a network to share guest information. Such a web would allow the Mexico City property to give a Canadian guest the same recognition received at the Toronto hotel. Setting up such a network is not simple. Arranging for dedicated lines is complicated and expensive. Moreover, the company is finding inconsistent crossover patterns. While many guests of the Four Seasons Toronto Hotel also stay at the Vancouver property, guests at the Philadelphia hotel don't frequent other Four Seasons' properties. Such stay patterns must be researched before an efficient network can be designed.

Guest Profiles for Restaurants

Micro-market segmentation, which is at the root of all successful guest-profile programs, is now available for many types of food-service operations. Today's electronic technology, including satellite-based communication networks, allows retailers to track their customers' lifestyles and buying habits. Supermarket retailers were the first to realize the technology's potential, and have since pioneered sophisticated systems for point-of-sale database marketing.

MerchanTec International, an Atlanta-based company, introduced a food-service database marketing system at the National Restaurant Association trade show earlier this year. MerchanTec calls it new system "InstAward," and claims it as the only commercially available service of its kind for restaurants and quick-service retail chains. InstAward lets participating food-service operators issue magnetic strip "Loyalty" cards to their frequent customers, thereby allowing the stores to identify and monitor customers' buying patterns.

To enroll in the program, the consumer completes an application at a participating unit. Once the application is processed by MerchanTec, an electronic file is created, which stores specific demographic and psychographic data, such as addresses, purchasing habits, and personality traits (e.g. food preferences, dining-out habits), and additional personal information such as birth dates and anniversaries. Then the customer is issue the encoded card.

Afterward, when the member-consumer makes a purchase, the customer accrues "Points" or other loyalty awards by presenting the card and swiping it through an electronic terminal. For the consumer, the appeal of a program such as this is that discounts and awards can be taken advantage of immediately.

For the retailer, or food-service operator, the major benefit is a database of consumer profiles that is essential to micro-market segmentation and effective direct marketing. By tracking customers' buying habits, businesses can know almost immediately when there's a disruption in those habits, and can respond to their best patrons' needs and preferences. Moreover, retailers and restauranteurs will no longer have to bother with coupon offers. Discounts and meal promotions can be keyed to the members' cards.

For corporations that operated in a variety of fast-food segments (such as PepsiCo, with its pizza, burger, Mexican, and Chicken brands), providing consumers with an InstAward-type incentive to patronize its outlets is a way to capture business that otherwise might go to a competitor. It's likely that, just as frequent flyers tend to be loyal to the airline with which they have accumulated the most points, fast-food customers will become loyal to those restaurants that offer some sort of "bonus" program.

An added benefit, according to <u>American Demographics</u> (January, 1991), is that properly constructed data-based marketing "can reduce the cost of marketing by increasing marketing's precision," an important consideration for an industry that traditionally has relied on mass-marketing to lure fickle and finicky customers to the cash register.

"New-Fashioned" Service

Overall, using new technology to manage guest information will restore the personal touch that technology is often accused of destroying. Guest recognition will allow hotels and restaurants to maintain close customer relationships based on personalized service. Such relationship management will keep customers coming back.

EXERCISE

1.   What are the issues that these "Guest History" systems seem to be addressing?

2.   What are some of the risks involved in this technology? Are there privacy issues that must be considered? Consider the differences between guest perceptions of privacy invasion and the actual realities of these systems.

3.   Discuss the possibility of data corruption, inaccurate data, and potential embarrassment for the service establishments as well as the customers.

4.   Discuss the issue of rising customer expectations as they become aware that you have this data available.

5.   What are the possible legal issues involved in maintaining and using such data as has been described in these cases?

CASE 9
INTERNATIONAL BUSINESS MACHINES[1]

IBM began as the Computing-Tabulation-Recording Company in 1914. In 1924, it adopted the name of International Business Machines. Since then, it has been enjoying a reputation for technological leadership, growing with the rest of the computer industry.

"Big Blue", as IBM has been known, is in the business of applying advanced information technology to solve problems involving human activities for business, governments, science, space exploration, defense, education, and medicine. It incorporates information processing systems, software, communications systems and other products and services in configurations to make possible comprehensive solutions that respond to customers' information needs. Its customers range from individuals considering a first computer to multinational companies searching for solutions on a global scale. Each has a specific need, and IBM's objective is to provide solutions to problems across the entire continuum.

IBM participates in different market sectors in the local as well as the global computer industry. Statistics for revenues and market share in mainframes, minicomputers, microcomputers, peripherals, and other categories are contained in the accompanying tables. IBM is number one in most of the categories, but is not a leader in two of the fastest growing categories, laptops and technical workstations.

---

[1]   This case was written by William C. House, University of Arkansas and Walter E. Greene, The University of Texas-Pan American. Published with the permission of the North American Case Research Association.

For the past two decades, the computer industry has been characterized by rapid change. In order to respond to ever increasing competition, IBM restructured its operations in January 1988, shifting from a product-oriented to a market-oriented approach striving to reunite estranged product development and marketing arms and to minimize the common practice of creating products in a vacuum.

A Marketing Perspective

As of 1989, IBM had more than 5 million customers all around the world. Geographic areas are covered by four major organizational units, including IBM U.S., IBM World Trade Americas, World Trade Asia/Pacific, and IBM World Trade Europe/Middle East/Africa.

IBM's marketing and service operations continue to enhance the company's working relationships with customers, focusing on better understanding of their needs and responding to these needs quickly, efficiently, and in a cost-effective manner. In 1987, IBM began a series of forums for customers, inviting customers to participate in its strategic product planning process. These forums provide IBM executives with an opportunity to discuss current product strategies and business directions, as well as to obtain feedback and suggestions from customers in developing future products.

IBM also expanded its field marketing force to increase the company's coverage in customer accounts by adding more than 1500 marketing representatives and systems engineers worldwide in the last two years. In response to expansion and a market driven strategy, IBM has invested substantial sums and time on education programs and sales training programs throughout the world. These training programs sharpened specialized skills of its field sales and support workers. IBM, as a single company in the computer industry, is now targeting some 250 industries.

Another important move was the adoption of a branch-level revenue-based compensation system for sales representatives. Beginning in January 1990, the performance of IBM's field managers and sales representatives was to be measured on the basis of total revenue brought into the company from any source (e.g., hardware, software, operational services) and not on total unit sales.

In 1988, the company expanded its Business Partner Program to include remarketers, dealers, and agents who sell selected IBM products, or complement IBM products and services with their own products in addressing specific customer needs. It also implemented the industry's most aggressive alliance-building efforts. IBM is now linked with a broad range of independent software vendors and large customers willing to tailor key tools and applications across its major computing environments. This move was aimed at providing more customer solutions, thereby increasing the quantity and quality of applications and other tools running on IBM systems as well as broadening industry support for SAA. So far, support for SAA has been slow to materialize.

Development centers have been established in countries to bring customers, IBM Business Partners, and IBM account teams together to customize and develop new applications for use on IBM systems. The company also continues to focus on ways to make it easier for customers to do business using IBM Link, an on-line electronic support service that facilitates customer efforts to obtain information on IBM's products and services.

Management Perspective--The New IBM

The Chairman of IBM's board, J. F. Akers, admitted that IBM has been slow to address changing market needs. He said in August 1989, "We took our eyes off the ball." He also conceded that the company was too "preoccupied with product competitiveness when competition heated up during the 70's and 80's." In 1989, Akers also announced two key goals for IBM: a 20% profit margin and 20% return on investment. Taking into account current operating results, IBM executives say that the current goal is a return on investment of 18 percent. This would allow the company to achieve revenue growth of 5 to 10%, to meet capital and dividend needs, and to maintain a balanced product line.

To enhance responsiveness to customers, IBM restructured its operations in 1988 to better control costs and expenses and to streamline its product offerings. It established seven lines of business (LOBs), each with decentralized decision-making and product responsibility. The goal was to reduce new product development times and improve working relations with customers. These LOBs were given responsibility for worldwide development and manufacturing operations in the U.S. as well as for revenue and profitability goals of their products and services. Unit managers report to a single executive, Terry Lautenbach, at IBM U.S. Headquarters.

There are occasional clashes between LOBs, according to some IBM executives. For example, there was intense debate between the Application Business Systems (ABS) LOB and the Personal Systems (PS) LOB in regard to the low end portion of IBM's midrange processor strategy due to the fact that ABS owns the AS/400 midrange product while PS was updating its own RT workstation line to overlap the low end of the AS/400 product line. Turf battles as well as technological problems have delayed the introduction of new versions of IBM's 9370 midrange processor. "But we know how to sit down and we're friends enough to able to argue about it when we have to and to come to a resolution," Carl J. Conti, Enterprise Systems LOB general manager, acknowledged.

Vice President Terry R. Lautenbach had been playing the role of judge and jury in such disputes to make sure that the various groups were not working at cross purposes. To promote cooperation, Lautenbach had identified key technologies that should be of concern to all product groups and assigned one LOB executive to be responsible for coordinating development of each key technology.

Akers' Comments on Current Company Status

John Akers, frustrated by IBM's less than spectacular showing in a rapidly changing computer industry during the late 1980's, let loose a tirade at a management meeting in April 1991. He remarked that employees had become too comfortable at the world's largest computer hardware company and that too many individuals were standing around waiting to be told what to do. In effect, too much time was being spent in talking rather than carrying out assigned tasks. Those who are in selling should sell and those who are in manufacturing should build. He called performance in both the U.S. and Japan unsatisfactory, based on the idea that if the company is not keeping pace then that is unsatisfactory performance. Going further, he stated flatly, "If any of our people can't be competitive and change as fast as the industry, then it's goodbye".

Noting that the U.S. salesforce had increased 25% from 20,000 to 25,000 since 1986, but U.S. sales revenues had increased less than 7% during the last half of the 1980's, Akers asked, "Where's the return to the company for hiring 5,000 extra people. Worldwide, IBM revenues are now 21% of total computer industry revenues compared to 30% in 1985. The fact that we are losing market share makes me *#* *.*# mad." He noted that the computer business is growing at a rate of 10% worldwide while IBM is growing at a slower rate. Akers has strongly asserted that he intends to turn the company around, one way or the other, by the time he is expected to retire in 1995.

A survey of IBM employees indicates that about 50% of those surveyed said many employees don't work hard enough and managers often don't try to motivate employees, but concentrate on protecting their own positions. In fact, inside and outside observers have criticized the company for keeping marginal performers on the job far too long. One software developer who now works for Microsoft observed that IBM has a bad habit of holding marathon meetings which often don't accomplish very much. A chip designer criticizes Akers for not accepting responsibility, while blaming the rank and file for declining profits and market share. Some workers are also upset at Akers' language. Several employees have also been critical of the 138% increase in salary and bonus which Akers received in 1990 at a time when the company was experiencing lay-offs and profit declines.

Using an electronic forum or bulletin board which allowed users to attach comments to electronically stored documents, a number of IBM employees responded to Akers comments. These comments indicated that many employees think senior executives are out of touch, that cooperation between divisions is rare, and that IBM is selling high-priced low-quality products.

The current system is seen to reward non-technical managers who concentrate on empire building and neglect to report bad news to higher-ups. Overemphasis on cost cutting and maximizing short term revenues appears to jeopardize long term, strategic projects. More rapid product prototyping is needed, in the view of many employees, involving customers in early versions of products before they are refined. It is not uncommon for IBM personnel to propose solutions for problems which exceed customer budgets by substantial amounts, while competitors propose solutions which do not exceed budgetary limitations.

Employee recommendations-including making it mandatory for development groups to use modern computing and communication tools-are being encouraged. Less attention should be paid to marketing to computer professionals, and more should be paid to reducing management levels, so there is more contact between top or middle management levels and non-management employees. Above all, the pace of project completion should be speeded up, so that a six month project doesn't take five years to complete.

Other Organizational and Strategic Moves

To sharpen its focus on the core business of computers and communications, IBM sold its copier sales and services operations as well as its educational publishing subsidiary in 1988. The company was also spending more money on software development than hardware development in 1988 and 1989, with that trend to continue into the 1990's.

Another move was to cut prices. For example, in the spring of 1989, IBM responded to Amdahl and Hitachi's mainframe competition by offering its mainframes at prices up to 25% off. It reacted to a sluggish market situation in the fourth quarter of 1989 with another massive restructuring of field operations to eliminate 10,000 more jobs from the U.S. work force and to slash one billion dollars from operating costs. This move was expected to boost earnings by $1.00 per share starting in 1990, according to John F. Akers. In 1990, the goal was to cut 14,000 employees. Since 1986, the company has reduced its workforce standing to about 373,000 persons. Some analysts feel that IBM must make future cuts in the number of employees and operating costs before earnings will increase significantly, pointing out that IBM geared up to meet its goal of becoming a $100 billion dollar company by 1990 and has fallen short of that goal by one-third.

Other strategic moves include introduction of new SAA based environments and aggressively pushing a wider range of operational services such as data center management. To fight the "open system attack" IBM made a two-pronged response. One aspect was to emphasize "Office Vision " a software bridge that straddled its three architectures--personal computers, minicomputers, and mainframes. The other aspect was to join these architectures with IBM's version of UNIX called AIX, allowing IBM machines to be connected to competitors' hardware.

IBM's efforts to improve customer responsiveness did not pay off in revenue growth from software and services in the third and fourth quarters of 1989. One reason was IBM's failure to ship the 3390 large disk files when expected. In addition, some customers were still unsure of the company's ability to deliver key products to the market in a timely fashion. Furthermore, users were often unwilling to turn over the responsibility for developing and managing information systems (IS) to any outside entity. The ability to deliver business solutions to customer problems is still an IBM weak point, although most observers say the technical support is very good.

Mainframe Reorientation Program

James Cannavino, a veteran mainframe computer engineer, was assigned to take charge of all personal computer operations in December 1988. He replaced William Lowe, who was overseer for the development of the first personal computer prototype. Lowe resigned to take a senior position at Xerox Corporation. Some analysts see the arrival of Cannavino as part of an IBM PC strategy called cooperative processing, which would involve connecting PCs to mainframes to allow smaller computers to draw on the storage capacities and computer power of the largest systems.

An integral part of the strategy is replacing existing PCs with PS/2s requiring OS/2 operating systems. In many ways, OS/2 resembles the core software of IBM mainframes. So far, OS/2 sales have been slow, but are expected to increase in the next two to three years. Microsoft 's Windows environment used in conjunction with DOS has proven to be far more popular than OS/2 with its presentation manager.

Demand for mainframes has fallen drastically as computing tasks are being moved to smaller machines. Between 1975 and 1988 mainframe sales declined from 78% to 35% of total U.S. computer hardware sales, but mainframe sales revenues increased overall. At present, IBM obtains about one-half of its revenues and two-thirds of its profits from mainframe sales. It has about 2/3 of the mainframe market, but only about 20% of the personal computer market.

IBM is making major price cuts in mainframes to counter competition from such suppliers as Amdahl and Hitachi. IBM's discounting has had little impact on market share but has hurt company profitability. Discounts have also diverted attention from service and focused on price as the primary sales appeal. Such moves also have provided competitors with a better chance to compete on equal terms with IBM.

Customers now appear to desire open systems, a configuration which would allow them to use their own programs on a variety of different manufacturers' hardware. Switching suppliers and connecting different suppliers' hardware is often inhibited by existing incompatibilities. IBM is now striving to improve connectability among its own computers while discouraging customers from switching to other suppliers.

IBM has experienced delays in new product introductions due to its slow, deliberate style. Market researchers often spend months in defining markets, with additional delays occurring to ensure that all projects approved pass a compatibility test with other lines. It can take 30 to 36 months for the process to be completed. Company executives say that IBM's size requires that it take the time necessary to manufacture a product.

David Hultman of System One says that IBM is too slow in responding to customer requests because field representatives have to go through too many management levels. A survey of 50 users indicates that while IBM is striving to become more flexible, it still often moves too slowly to meet customer needs.

A good example of the slow pace of product introductions is IBM's new laptop computer. While receiving good marks from users in technologically sophisticated environments, it appears to be priced too high to be a serious factor in the small business and educational markets, although it sells well to large accounts. At $5,995, IBM's laptop costs about $2,500 more than comparable Dell or AST models.

The introduction of the personal computer in 1981 has proved to be a mixed blessing for IBM. Until then, the company controlled information systems design in a vast majority of companies. Customers rarely bought systems software unless it was compatible with IBM machines. Instead of retaining its control over core software interfaces and connections, IBM farmed out the operating system development to Microsoft. The widespread availability of MS/DOS opened the way for development channels. In its first year of operation, the company bureaucracy still works to inhibit individual initiative and often alienates customers.

IBM has announced that a new family of mainframes called Summit won't be introduced until late 1991. However, the expected introduction of an improved mainframe by Hitachi may impact IBM's current plans. Some improvements in speeding up 3090 software and introducing faster, fiber optic input/output channels were made in 1990. Faster I/O channels now permit customers to locate disk drives miles away instead of only 400 feet in the past.

IBM expects to ship some small versions of its new mainframe in September 1991. Analysts believe there are at least 300 firm orders for the ES/9000 series representing about four and one-half billion dollars in revenue, with the possibility of selling at least 150 more if plant capacity were available.

Among competitors, Digital Equipment has become the number two computer maker by virtue of marketing small, medium sized computers that work together easily and use the same software. The introduction of the VAX 9000 in late 1989 provided DEC with a price/performance edge over IBM'S five year old 3090 product line. Richard Whitmen, Digital Equipment Marketing Manager, said that the new VAX 9000 configuration would cost half as much as a comparable 3090 system and an Aberdeen Group computer analyst said that DEC can connect its machine to IBM mainframes more easily than IBM. DEC stands to benefit from a current trend toward employing networks of computers that distribute computing jobs and perform on line transactions processing. It is not likely to replace many 3090's because of the difficulties and costs of hardware and software conversions.

In 1990, 44% of IBM's revenues came from mainframe sales, with 21% from mid-range computers, 18% from personal computers and 17% from software, leasing, and other sources. IBM's share of the mainframe market declined from 53% in 1989 to 50.7% in 1990. The expected fourth quarter upsurge in revenues from mainframe sales is not likely to increase total revenues significantly because of a stronger dollar in foreign markets where IBM obtains 60% of its business and because of economic declines being experienced in many countries where IBM has a strong presence.

Industry Trends: A Switch from Mainframe to Micros

The mainframe computer business has been hard hit in recent years by increasing consumer preference for smaller, more powerful computers including personal computers and computer workstations. From 1983 to 1988, mainframe shipments declined 20% while personal computer shipments have increased 59% and workstation shipments have increased from 3500 to 180,000 units. The Computer and Business Equipment Manufacturers Association predicts that unit mainframe sales will only increase 2.6% annually while personal computer sales will increase 14.5% annually from 1990 to 1998. Many analysts predict laptop computer models will outsell desktop models by a margin of at least two to one. In some cases, networks of personal computers turn out to be cheaper and can perform the same jobs better than mainframes.

A frequently cited advantage of personal computer networks is lower costs, including hardware, software, and personnel. For example, Consolidated Insurance is converting from a $3 million IBM mainframe to a $300,000 network of personal computers, thereby reducing its data processing staff from 30 to 10 persons and operating costs by one million dollars. Such longtime mainframe users as Playboy Enterprises, Hiram Walker, Kaiser Aluminum, U. S. Shoe, Harley Davidson, Arco Chemical, Colgate Palmolive, and Johnson and Johnson are moving to replace IBM mainframes with minicomputers such as the AS/400 series. Several other organizations (e.g., Georgia Pacific and Pepperidge Farms) have switched to a combination of minicomputers and personal computers.

William Zachman says that the computer industry is in the throes of a major change in economics with ominous implications for mainframe suppliers, while NCR Chairman Charles Exley asserts that microprocessor-based systems have at least a 100 to one cost advantage over mainframes which can only increase over time. Mainframe customers are rapidly becoming aware of this cost differential.

Many data processing managers, raised in mainframe environments, are resisting the downsizing movement in order to preserve their present positions and avoid losing staff. Some companies with large databases would find it difficult to break them into smaller chunks that could be handled by PC networks. IBM executives hotly dispute any notion of a mainframe demise, claiming that most personal computers don't have the processing power and storage capacity to manage large databases. Furthermore, they point out that large systems have fast communication channels and facilitate automatic backup. In addition, large mainframe makers will find it difficult to generate enough revenues from PC network configurations to support large sales and service support organizations.

Don Young, Sanford C. Berstein and Company analyst, points out that personal computers cannot process large amounts of data and move the volumes involved through networks of small computers as fast as mainframes can. Therefore, the explosion in the number of personal computers may well create large volumes of data which can only be handled by mainframes.

Revenue and Profit Position

In 1989, U.S. revenues of IBM increased only by 1.5% to $25.7 billion whereas international revenues increased 7.6% to $36 billion. IBM expected sales revenues to increase about 8% in 1990. Profit margins have been squeezed by fierce competition in the markets which IBM serves. In 1989, profits declined $800 million below 1984 levels, or 35% from 1988, to $3.8 billion. Akers says a key company goal is to push company operating margins back up to at least 18% of sales revenues. Lower costs will help in international more than in the more saturated, highly competitive domestic markets. About two thirds of 1990 net income was derived from international operations, especially Europe and Eastern markets where IBM has a dominant position.

In 1990, total company sales increased 10% over 1989 levels and net income increased 60% compared to paltry profit levels of 1989. However, revenues for the first quarter of 1991 were $13.5 billion, down almost 5% from a year earlier. The company actually experienced its first quarterly loss of almost $2 billion due largely to an unexpected accounting loss. Results for the second quarter were expected to be down from the second quarter of 1990. Estimated earnings for 1991 are $4 billion compared to $6 billion in 1990. IBM still has not reached the profit levels of $6.6 billion attained in 1984 on revenues of $46 billion. By comparison, in 1990, net profits were $6 billion produced by revenues of $69 billion.

In an effort to reduce costs and improve profitability, the company has cut the number of employees by more than 25,000 since 1986. In January of 1990, IBM announced a work force reduction of 10,000 employees. So far, the employee reduction campaign has made only a small dent in sales and administrative expenses. These costs are 30% of revenues at IBM compared to 25% revenues at similar computer hardware companies. As a first step, IBM will likely lower prices further and extend discounts. If these actions are not successful in increasing revenues and profits, further plant closings and layoffs are considered likely by the mid-1990's. Some analysts say the company needs to cut at least 30,000 more employees in order to restore profits to desired levels.

IBM continues to make significant long term investments, especially in R & D outlays ($5.9 billion), plant and other property ($ 4.4 billion) and capitalized costs of software products ($1.3 billion). These investments have provided the company with the technology and capacity for growth to enable it to compete more effectively in its environment.

IBM fought encroachments on its installed hardware base by developing more complex and sophisticated computing systems. This approach is no longer acceptable to many users who want the ability to mix and match components from different vendors.

IBM is on the horns of a dilemma in balancing shareholder and customer needs. The open systems desired by many customers have lower profit margins than proprietary products and will likely result in lower earnings levels. On the other hand, pursuing higher margin, proprietary systems will eventually result in further loss of market share and long term earnings losses. IBM also has large numbers of personnel who have worked in mainframes their entire careers and are now faced with distribution environments which require a completely different approach. The requirements for host based open systems with distributed networks are likely to be completely different than those for customers with large mainframes seeking cooperative processing systems.

EXERCISE

1.   What product lines and markets should IBM emphasize in the future in order to maintain its competitive position in the computer hardware industry?

2.   In the 1980s, IBM set goals of attaining $100 billion in sales revenue and achieving return on sales and return on investment of 20%. Are these realistic goals, and if so, how can IBM best attain them?

3.   Evaluate the position of IBM in the industry in terms of such measures as sales and income growth, sales and income per employee, net income/sales, and R&D outlays. What are the implications of this analysis?

TABLE 1
SALES, INCOME, AND ASSET GROWTH FOR COMPUTER COMPANIES

Company	Sales Growth		Income Growth		Asset Growth	
	90/89	89/88	90/89	89/88	90/89	89/88
APPLE	1.07	1.21	1.14	1.05	1.12	1.24
AMDAHL	1.03	1.17	1.20	0.76	1.04	1.16
COMPAQ	1.25	1.39	1.36	1.31	1.30	1.31
DEC	1.01	1.05	1.00	0.72	1.03	1.10
HEW PCKRD	1.10	1.20	0.95	0.97	1.09	1.31
IBM	1.10	1.05	1.60	0.68	1.13	1.06
NCR	1.06	0.99	0.90	0.94	1.01	0.95
SUN MCRSYS	1.35	1.41	318.00	0.40	1.49	1.50
UNISYS	1.00	1.02	0.00	0.00	0.96	0.97
WANG	0.87	0.90	0.00	0.00	0.72	0.83
Average	1.08	1.05	*0.77	0.68	1.09	1.14

*Does not include Sun Microsystems.

TABLE 2
SALES, INCOME, AND ASSETS PER EMPLOYEE

Company	Sales/Employee		Income/Employee		Asset/Employee	
	1990	1989	1990	1989	1990	1989
APPLE	451.6	423.8	38.6	34.6	235.7	221.9
AMDAHL	255.1	257.1	21.1	18.7	264.3	273.3
COMPAQ	317.5	367.4	39.9	42.6	312.8	267.0
DEC	105.5	104.6	0.6	7.1	93.5	91.0
HEW PCKRD	143.8	135.7	8.0	8.9	123.9	112.1
IBM	184.6	162.8	16.1	9.8	234.2	201.8
NCR	116.3	102.7	6.7	7.1	81.8	77.6
SUN MCRSYS	215.7	198.6	9.6	3.5	156.5	140.7
UNISYS	134.3	115.2	(5.8)	(7.3)	136.7	122.7
WANG	131.0	92.5	(35.6)	(18.1)	94.5	85.0
Average	205.5	196.0	9.9	10.7	173.4	159.3

TABLE 3
RETURN ON SALES AND R&D$/SALES

Company	Net Income/Sales Revenues			R&D Outlays/Sales Revenues		
	1987	1988	1989	1987	1988	1989
APPLE	9.21	9.45	8.15	6.7	7.2	6.7
AMDAHL	9.43	17.3	7.61	12.3	11.9	12.3
COMPAQ	11.1	12.3	11.6	4.3	3.8	3.6
DEC	12.4	9.84	6.77	10.7	10.8	11.4
HEW PCKRD	8.27	8.06	6.55	11.6	11.1	10.4
IBM	9.70	9.20	5.99	7.8	7.4	7.4
NCR	7.46	7.33	6.92	6.6	6.3	7.0
SUN MCRSYS	6.34	11.9	1.75	6.6	6.3	7.0
UNISYS	5.95	6.88	NEG.	5.9	6.1	7.2
WANG	3.10	1.63	NEG.	7.7	7.9	8.7
Average	8.30	9.39	6.92	8.8	8.5	8.8

Source: Business Week 1000, 1990, 1989; Forbes 500, 1990, 1989

TABLE 4
IBM CORPORATION GROSS PROFITS FOR 1989 AND 1990

Product Category	1989 Gross Profits		1990 Gross Profits	
	Million$	Percent	Million$	Percent
Mainframe Hardware, Software, Peripherals, and Maintenance	18,083	49.2	19,087	49.8
Midrange Hardware	3,004	8.2	2,339	6.1
Non-Mainframe Peripherals	2,379	6.5	2,020	5.3
Personal Computers, Terminals, Workstations, and Typewriters	6,249	17.0	7,089	18.5
Non-Mainframe Software and Maintenance	4,964	13.5	4,757	12.4
Other	2,102	5.7	3,030	7.9
Totals	36,781	100.0	38,321	100.0

Source: Sanford G. Bernstein, Business Week, March 29, 1989, p. 72 and June 17, 1991, p. 29.

TABLE 5
IBM REVENUES AND NET INCOME FOR 1989 THROUGH 1992

Revenues (Billions $)	62.7	69.0	65.0	71.5
Net Income (Millions $)	5,251	6,020	2,755	4,920

Source: Value Line Investment Service, 1991.

Case 10
JOHN'S PHARMACY[1]

A blond, slightly bald man in his forty's stood paralyzed before a $10,000 CRT screen waiting rigidly for the menu to give him the next command. Finally, the instruction "Caution-Reaction" appeared on the screen. The pharmacist, looking up from the screen, observed many customers waiting impatiently for their prescriptions. Panic-stricken, he reached for the procedures manual, a monstrous book with numerous tabs sticking out of it.

Again he glanced nervously at the customers who were becoming more and more restless as each moment passed. He began to thumb through the procedures manual to find what this never before encountered message on the screen meant.

He thought, "How could a manual be so hard to read? I am an educated man with a degree in biology and pharmacology and I can't even find the right section of the manual. I don't need this type of aggravation. I'm only working here as a relief man so John, the owner, can have some days off. Where is Alice? She is the only other person who knows the system. When will she get back from lunch?"

Finally, he found the chapter of the manual entitled "Drug Reaction". Quickly he read the instructions, realizing that the customer line was becoming longer. The manual instructed him to look in another section of the manual to find out what type of reaction might happen. Luckily, the reaction wasn't severe and could be overridden.

---

[1]   This case was written by John C. Malley, University of Central Arkansas and Alice Robertson, Trover Clinic.

Instantly he flipped to the first section and looked for the next instruction. The manual instructed him to "strike F6 to override".

Immediately, the pharmacist struck the F key, then the 6 key. Still the screen displayed the "Caution-Reaction" warning. Again, this time with rage and anger, the pharmacist typed F and then 6. Again no response. The frustration and irritation raged inside the pharmacist, "This 8?[* machine."

After Alice arrived back from lunch, she noticed a long line at the pharmacy counter. As she walked closer, Alice saw the panic in the relief pharmacist's eyes. As their eyes met, Alice began to worry and thought to herself, "What could have happened to him to make him so far behind waiting on customers?"

"The *?~* machine is frozen," he said (away from earshot range of the customers) as Alice entered the pharmacy. Alice looked at the screen and then pressed the Function 6 key. The CRT responded with "Override Complete".

Again the relief man uttered 4-letter word, "Why didn't that *?!* manual just tell me to push the function 6 keys?"

Alice's reply was, "Because a computer person wrote the manual."

This scenario occurred after the installation of a computer system in a one-owner pharmacy. The benefits of the system were very obvious; all the operations in the entire pharmacy were reduced to fit on a floppy disk system. Information was available at his finger tips if the pharmacist could only discover its secrets hidden in the user manual.

There were many more of these pathetic scenes in the following months. The manual became more and more useless and unserviceable. Instructions were written for the computer literate, the pharmacy personnel were still a part of the unsaved computer illiterates. Oh sure, they could throw around words like bytes, software, and hardware. However, countless times dictionaries were consulted so that they could understand the instructions.

Once, after numerous attempts to enter a new file without success, they knew that they must read the manual. By this time they were using the massive document as a step ladder. Alice dragged and pulled and tugged until she finally had it back in the pharmacy. The hideous manual sent a shiver of dread through her as she searched for the correct section. Minutes passed and the section could not be found. Alice looked up at John, the owner, and saw the all too familiar look of fear.

He then said what she dreaded to hear, "We will have to call the company."

"Oh! No!", she thought to herself. "Talking to a computer programmer on the phone is worse than reading this manual."

"Let me have one more try at finding it," she said as she probed through the manual. However, the attempted search was abandoned and the phone call was made.

John began the conversation with the company and explained what happened. The man on the other line immediately began using fourteen letter words that John had never heard before. He motioned for Alice to pick up on the extension and as she did she wondered what language the man was speaking. Then Alice recognized it; the words were from a COBOL book that she had while taking a computer course in college. Alice had seen the words before in print, but didn't realize that anyone would actually use them in daily conversation. Eventually, the problem was solved by rebooting the system.

EXERCISES

1. Assume you are John, the owner of the pharmacy. What immediate actions could you take to help relieve the day-to-day frustrations encountered in using the system?

2. Assume you are the product manager for the software product in the case. What are your responsibilities for user training, system implementation, and problem solving?

3. Develop an analysis discussing the roles a tutorial program, a quick reference list, common error codes list, and list of key terms could have had in resolving these difficulties?

CASE 11
KATCO AND ORGANIZATIONAL POLITICS[1]

One of the fastest, simplest, and least expensive ways to communicate internationally is through the use of electronic mail services to transmit standard electronic mail messages over private (leased) telecommunications networks and provide gateways to dial automatically into international public electronic mail networks. Such a system was implemented at KATCO and led to conflict between subsidiaries and departments of this international company. All the participants tried to dominate and control the implementation and management of the technology.

Background

These electronic mail systems provide a variety of new time-saving features. Full-function word processing software for creating and editing messages replaced older data entry technology; abbreviated routing codes were defined in the system to simplify dialing of frequently called numbers and associated "answer-back" or security codes; and electronic filing allowed online retrieval and inspection of messages.

The system could collect and "batch" messages to a destination for immediate or delayed delivery. It could hold messages for delivery at a later time, or it could automatically redial busy destinations periodically until the connection had been established. These features were particularly important for firms communicating to countries with unreliable electronic communications capabilities.

---

[1] This case was written by Charlene A. Dykman and Charles K. Davis, University of Houston-Downtown

KATCO hoped to save money through the use of private leased-lines to send messages through Amsterdam and on to their ultimate destinations at vastly lower rates than sending the same message from the United States using dial-up long distance calling. Multinational companies that used electronic mail heavily for communication with clients, suppliers, and job sites saw enormous potential benefits from these computerized capabilities. In many such companies, electronic mail-based communications were generally viewed as an administrative service, closely related to ordinary telephone services. Electronic mail was not associated with the computing function in these organizations and it was the administrative services area in these multinationals that frequently pursued acquisition of this mail technology.

KATCO is a multinational "infrastructure" construction firm, that designs and builds bridges, dams, roads and highways. Headquartered in Chicago, Katco's revenues exceed a billion dollars annually, mostly from construction projects at remote locations in the Middle East and the Far East. The principal means of communication with foreign customers, suppliers, partners, and remote site employees is by electronic mail.

Each of KATCO's main offices and construction sites employed a staff of mail system operators to support international communications requirements based upon standard international network protocols. Operators communicated with remote locations using point-to-point dial-up telephone links to transmit messages. The process of handling each electronic mail message was slow and laborious.

As technology became available, an analysis of the potential savings associated with implementing a computer-based electronic mail message switch at KATCO was performed. It was determined that a switch would be located in Amsterdam with the Director of Administrative Services responsible for its operation and maintenance.

The Implementation

KATCO's message-switching electronic mail system was a stand-alone computer application that was introduced into an established work group of non-technical, low-level, key-entry clerks who lacked notable computing experience. With this system, these workers were required to interface directly with a computer system that was integral to success in performing work assignments.

A corporate staff member in Chicago selected the system and directed the implementation at the Amsterdam subsidiary. Selection and acquisition followed procedures appropriate for telephone system acquisitions. The electronic mail function was managed by the administrative services area at KATCO where responsibility for the telephone system also resided, and the electronic mail technology being replaced was regarded as one of the telephone services. Computing, and the data communications activities associated with computing, reported into a separate functional area. The methodology used to acquire the first switch included these steps:

o   A major vendor of KATCO's electronic mail services in Chicago provided administrative management with technical contacts who promoted the technology.

o   That vendor presented the product concept and described the key features of its own planned electronic mail system products.

o   Competing vendors were identified and their products examined to determine if prices and features were competitive.

o   A list of features needed was compiled after interviews with electronic mail supervisors in Chicago and Amsterdam offices of KATCO.

o   A "Request for Proposal" was prepared.

o   Features of each vendor's proposed switch were compared.

o   Financial analysis was performed, a recommendation was made to administrative management and a system was selected.

o   A standard contract for acquisition and maintenance was executed.

o   The switch was installed in Amsterdam and operators were given on-the-job training.

o   The other offices of KATCO were sent instructions regarding access and use of the Amsterdam system.

The implementation did not go well. The vendor (a major American multinational firm) did not deliver the full-function switch as envisioned and instead provided a preliminary model of the switch on an "interim" basis. The software for this switch was unstable and unreliable. Technical and operational problems in the Amsterdam electronic mail room were soon disrupting electronic mail services worldwide.

A post-implementation review of the electronic mail system project was undertaken with the following observations:

o   The vendor had not delivered all of the features originally contracted.

o   Vendor maintenance was inadequate and not deemed responsive in handling time-critical problems.

o   No problem resolution procedures existed; operator, user support, computer, and networking problems were all handled ad hoc.

o   Documentation of the system's operation and the network configuration was missing or inadequate.

o   Operators did not trust the system; a vast majority of messages were being sent outside the system.

Clearly, the implementation of the electronic mail system had gone awry. KATCO was not able to realize the savings that could result from the use of the available unused capacity on its existing private data communications network to get messages to Amsterdam for subsequent retransmission. Similarly, they were not taking advantage of low European electronic mail rates that were the impetus for installation of the system in the first place.

EXERCISE

1.   What are the stages of the Systems Development Life Cycle that seem to have been overlooked in this project?

2.   You are the systems analyst who has been called in to consider the situation and to make a recommendation regarding replacement of the system. How would you proceed?

3.   What role do you think organizational politics has played in this failure? How would you address this?

4.   Develop an organizational matrix showing the types of responsibilities that various organizational players should have. For instance, who should choose the next vendor? Who should be responsible for the implementation and the ongoing management of the system?

CASE 12
KRUEPER ENGINEERING & ASSOCIATES, INC.[1]

In 1965 Harry Krueper and Robert Weddle founded Krueper (pronounce like "Creeper") Engineering and Associates, Inc. Due to family constraints, Robert Weddle did not remain in the business for long. Harry Krueper continued, and like many entrepreneurs had financial problems in the firm's early days. Later as the reputation of Krueper Engineering widened, the company began to thrive. The number of employees rose from about six in 1972 to 43 in 1988. The company has been in its present physical facility since 1972.

Krueper Engineering and Associates specializes in six specific types of consulting studies: land development, urban planning, land surveying, civil engineering, accident evaluation and traffic engineering. Local or state agencies are about thirty percent of their clients with developers, insurance companies, and attorneys as the rest.

The firm does no advertising. Yet, client growth is constant. Harry Krueper attributes demand for land analysis studies to the rapid expansion in the Inland Empire of Southern California. Others within the company attribute company growth to the outstanding reputation of Harry Krueper.

According to Harry Krueper, the most pressing issue facing his firm is the computerization of the accident reconstruction industry. Computers are revolutionizing his business. Some equipment (both hardware and software) was less than eight months

---

[1] The case was written by Sue Greenfeld, California State University, San Bernardino. Published with the permission of the North American Case Research Association.

old in 1988. Harry Krueper states that he is less enamored with computers than some of his employees, but he realizes that he must computerize to stay competitive.

An underlying, but equally important issue, is the management of growth, and Krueper's future as a sole proprietorship. Harry Krueper, as the company's only registered traffic engineer, provides 95% of the firm's expert testimony in court cases. Every traffic accident study must have his final approval. According to some employees, Krueper Engineering needs more people capable of delivering expert testimony in court. Some feel this is necessary for two reasons. First, to grow larger and second, to have a better control over the firm's backlog of accident reconstruction reports. "We have real growing pains," expressed one member of the company.

Company History

A framed newspaper clipping hangs in the reception hall at the present location announcing the original formation of Krueper Engineering in 1965. At that time, Harry Krueper joined surveyor Robert Weddle to open an office specializing in traffic engineering and land design. When the firm started, Harry Krueper was a Cal Poly Pomona engineering professor.

In the beginning, Krueper Engineering had the usual problems, both time and money, of an infant company trying to establish itself in a traditional market. Harry Krueper's first focus was on his teaching job and he devoted only part of his time to the company. Then in 1968 a geographical change caused additional strain within the firm. Weddle had moved to Apple Valley. This meant the two partners commuted about 40 miles one-way to provide their professional talent to each other.

Thus, to help the firm, Harry Krueper ended his teaching duties in 1970 to work full-time in the company. However, the geographical separation of the two partners continued to place pressure on the company. Finally in 1974, the partnership ended. Harry Krueper hired Carson Storer, a surveyor living in San Bernardino, to replace the services of Robert Weddle.

After 1970, the firm grew as a result of the increased importance of traffic planning and accident reconstruction, concepts of intensifying legal complexity. Many cities and public entities recognized the significance of traffic planning for reducing potential liability. New clients in Southern California and other western states spurred the enlargement of Krueper Engineering.

The firm earned a solid reputation for thoroughness in accident reconstruction and report preparation of a very high ethical standard. Krueper Engineering would not prepare a report which intentionally favored a client. The firm would present only the engineering facts, and these would be very carefully checked. Harry Krueper established himself as an expert witness in court testimony and cross examination. Accident reconstruction generated fifty percent of the annual workload handled by the firm by 1988. Harry Krueper currently holds engineering licenses in Arizona, California, Oregon and Nevada.

Company Mission

One employee when asked to define the mission of Krueper Engineering stated: "To provide the best service to our clients. That's it." Another person remarked, "I don't think where we are today was ever planned. I don't think any of us really wanted to reach this point."

A 1985 brochure puts the mission this way:

> Krueper Engineering is devoted to seeking the optimal balance between the needs of the human systems. This is achieved through creating innovative designs, as well as efficient solutions.

> Krueper Engineering has proven its proficiency in dealing with today's complex problems by providing dedicated, specialized assistance in over forty-five hundred jobs for over two thousand separate clients in both the public and private sector. With these requirements in mind, Krueper Engineering looks for the best people, then turns them loose on tough problems. They come up with solutions that work.

> Krueper Engineering's family begins with a staff of over 40, employing professional Civil Engineers, Land Surveyors, Traffic Engineers, and Land Planners. It is further diversified with highly qualified associates in Structural Engineering, Geology/Oils Engineering, Architecture, Landscape Architecture, Photogrammetry and other related areas. Together, they are capable of handling the widest possible range of client requests.

> With today's constantly changing social, economic, and physical environment, the primary objective of Krueper Engineering is to keep pace with these changes; thereby, achieving our goal of providing our clients with optimal solutions in their best interest, as well as promoting the public's health, safety and welfare.

Krueper Engineering has the capabilities to complete large scale projects, however, it is the objective of this company to ensure that every client, regardless of the size of the project, receives the attention and services on a personal, one-to-one basis."

Yet when asked to state a major objective of Krueper Engineering for five years hence, one person said, "to keep Harry Krueper alive."

Organizational Structure

Continued growth of Krueper Engineering caused problems in its structure and coordination. In 1987, Krueper Engineering decided to examine its organization structure. This led to the development of a formal organization chart which showed the flow of authority.

Carson Storer holds the second position of command as vice-president and principal surveyor. The remaining personnel are under six departments: engineering, land development, accident evaluation, planning, secretarial and bookkeeping. The first three functions contain the technical areas while the latter three provide support services to the firm.

Two individuals represent the engineering department which specializes in designs of subdivisions, sewers, and traffic systems. Fred Babbitt, a registered civil engineer, first became acquainted with Harry Krueper in 1970 while working as a systems analyst. After earning a civil engineering degree from Cal Poly Pomona in 1972, Babbitt began working full time for Krueper and remains in his position as project manager. He enjoys the freedom and flexibility of a small firm.

Originally, accident reconstruction used the services of the engineering department. As the workload increased, accident reconstruction became its own department. Engineering returned to traditional types of civil engineering projects.

Vice-President Carson Storer heads the land development department. He has one assistant surveyor and a field crew of five. Their surveying work concentrates on land use planning as well as the parcel map development for new subdivisions. Krueper Engineering no longer performs soil engineering due to the high level of specialization needed in this field.

The land development and accident reconstruction functions of Krueper remain separate entities with independent support staffs. Harry Krueper heads the accident reconstruction function as its chief principal civil and traffic engineer. John Toomey, an assistant engineer, coordinates the department's staff in gathering and condensing all the information required in each report. The division includes 23 other employees responsible for all phases required in the preparation of a complete legal engineering document.

Toomey's supervisory responsibilities include technical and design supervision. He supervises office technicians, office assistants, field crews, draftsmen, an illustrator (artist), a deposition researcher and a summarizer. Toomey has delegated much of his field and office supervisory duties to Shawn Grainger, a technical supervisor. This allows him more time to coordinate each final accident reconstruction presentation with Harry Krueper, Randy Frankie, and Loren Downard. Randy Frankie is a senior designer and Loren Downard is a traffic consultant.

Support functions of planning, secretarial, and bookkeeping have faced many challenges keeping up with the constant growth of Krueper Engineering. Gayle Champlain, supervisor of bookkeeping, noted that annual billings amounted to about $1.75 million in 1987 compared to $200,000 in 1973. Champlain has been responsible for changing the initial accounting methods. Simple bookkeeping procedures have been changed to a computerized system of tracing payments and balances.

Industry

Krueper Engineering provides six types of consulting studies; however, it has only two primary markets. One is accident evaluation and a second is civil engineering services. In the former, there is a consensus within the company that Krueper Engineering is unique. There are probably only four or five companies within the Western states capable of providing accident reconstruction work and only Krueper Engineering provides so complete an analysis. One individual stated that Krueper Engineering is number one in sales for this area.

On the other hand, the civil engineering market is very competitive. Over one hundred firms are capable of doing studies similar to Krueper Engineering. Land planning, land development, urban planning, and land surveying are interrelated. A problem occurs because the law states engineers and land surveyors cannot advertise. Thus, Krueper Engineering only lists their name in the yellow pages of the phone book.

Accident Reconstruction

Accident Reconstruction (the largest department with 23 people) is the heart of the company. The firm receives all its business through word of mouth built on the twenty-plus-year reputation of Harry Krueper. All employees agreed Krueper

Engineering attains more business in this area than they can handle. Clients, mostly attorneys and insurance agents, will call Krueper Engineering and seek an opinion about possible liability after an accident has occurred. Krueper Engineering does a complete study of the accident site including detailed drawings and analysis. These accidents usually involve some combination of automobiles, trucks, mopeds, and pedestrians. On a rare occasion, Krueper may cover the unusual accident such as when a customer slips and falls in a client's location. When a client calls in Krueper Engineering, the problem invariably concerns a very serious injury with medical complications.

In terms of overall causes of accidents, "driver inattention is probably one of the biggest factors in traffic accidents" states Harry Krueper. The other two major factors are road conditions and the vehicle involved.

Krueper Engineering actually goes on-site to the physical location where field employees take various measurements. Because safety of the field crew is a #1 concern, Krueper Engineering provides their personnel with orange roadvests, safety cones, and signs. In sixteen years of roadwork, Krueper Engineering reports no accidents involving their personnel.

Attention to safety can be especially important because night work is particularly hazardous. An accident which occurred at night must be analyzed under similar circumstances. Lights are checked according to city and county standards. Krueper Engineering measures the lights' high and low values. To get those values, personnel must stand in the road in darkness. Sometimes, they have to bend down to do work at ground level. On roads with heavy traffic volume, such measurements can possibly be quite dangerous. At least once a year, the issue of hazard pay arises from the field personnel because Krueper has no special issue compensation called "hazard pay." However, Carson Storer did not feel this was a significant issue.

Land Development

Krueper Engineering performs lot surveys from a single unit to a 200 industrial lot survey. If a developer has a 40-acre lot and wants to put 10 lots on it, Krueper Engineering could provide the land planning and layout. This would involve streets, grading, water and sewer plans. The major clients are developers, real estate agents, and individual property owners. Competitors vary in size. Some are one-person firms; others may have 14 or 15 engineers. Krueper Engineering considers itself as a medium size firm to offer land development services.

One major past project encompassed the mapping and the parceling of the land when Kaiser Steel went bankrupt. Another project included a parcel of 218 acres being developed into an industrial park.

Carson Storer stated that land development once generated about 50% of Krueper's revenue. Now, this area generates roughly 30%. He would like to see this area generate 50% of the revenue again. He feels land development could handle more work.

Stress and Work Overload

Employee stress and work overload is a major issue at Krueper Engineering. Several individuals stated they have more work than they can handle. One-third of the accident reconstruction reports have missed their due date because all the work cannot be completed on time. A client may wait nine months to one year to receive a report. Some clients call every other week to be sure their reports are given attention. There is a backlog of six months in accident reconstruction. Carson Storer indicated the "ideal" backlog would be one month for an accident reconstruction.

Part of the problem is a function of the personality of Harry Krueper. One employee stated Harry Krueper "doesn't have no in his vocabulary." Attorneys know if they call on Sunday, Harry Krueper will accept the job if he answers the phone. On the other hand, Harry Krueper commented the firm does turn work down. He refuses to accept business from lawyers he considers "unethical." However, he feels that about 70% of the lawyers are honest and ethical. Harry Krueper rarely turns down long-time clients. Krueper Engineering accepts about 85% of the inquiries into their firm.

Personnel Practices

Krueper Engineering offers a generous benefit package. This includes full medical coverage, life insurance, profit sharing, four week annual vacation allowances for long term employees, sick leave, holidays, flexible work hours, pregnancy leave, and travel expenses. Employees work four 10-hour-days, and many employees have been with the company for more than five years.

The firm schedules numerous company activities throughout the year to encourage the sense of belonging. Past outings have included golf tournaments, ski trips, picnics, camping trips, and Christmas parties. Carson Storer mentioned these group activities have built the company's dedication and tenacity. This helps the company succeed and has pulled Krueper through difficult periods in the past.

Raises are based on a performance evaluation and new employees will be on probation for three months. Wages are hourly, and a new person would probably start at $6 per hour, earning $7 per hour after three months and $10-$12 per hour after five years. One individual implied that wages at Krueper Engineering were better than average for comparable jobs elsewhere.

Everyone receives a raise if the company is doing well. For example, Krueper Engineering gave two across-the-board raises in 1988. Due to the financial health of the company, Krueper issued one raise in January and another in September. Employee turnover is greater than Krueper Engineering would like, but lower than that of other companies of comparable size.

Organizational Culture

The atmosphere of Krueper Engineering revolves around the tone set by Harry Krueper. He is the firm's only stockholder. He appears to make a concerted effort to create a family-type atmosphere.

Krueper Engineering faces many interpersonal challenges typical of small firms as they grow. One revolves around Harry Krueper, who wants to keep the high quality image by which Krueper Engineering is known. Employees describe Harry Krueper as "a brilliant, and ethical man of very high integrity," who also has compassion for his clients. He wants to charge very reasonable fees so the average person can afford his services. One board member stated they could easily double their "average" clientele. Another person described Harry Krueper as a minimalist or someone who wants or needs very little. However, there is a deep respect for Harry Krueper throughout the company.

Yet, frustration appears to exist under the surface. With fifteen employees, each felt they could have a special place with Harry Krueper, and they did. With forty-three employees, such is not the case. Harry Krueper is frequently out of the office testifying for various cases, as he is the firm's only expert witness. He relies on the reports produced by the firm, which he personally wants to review and supervise. He has not been able to relinquish control, especially in the accident reconstruction area. Sometimes he has overruled or undermined decisions of his managers and department heads. He has also accepted client work after others in the firm originally turned the work down. One individual described Harry Krueper as a "workaholic."

The responsibility for handling the day-to-day organizational climate rests with Carson Storer, appointed chief of personnel. He finds 75% of his time is spent in resolving personnel conflicts or promoting goodwill throughout the company. To illustrate, a recent incident provides a sign of how personnel issues consume his time. An issue arose because individuals taking soda cans from the refrigerator were not properly repaying the soda fund.

Two employees implied that acclimating to the structure of office politics was far more difficult for them than performing their duties. One mentioned that in 1987 a real morale problem existed. People felt there were unclear lines of command. Everyone thought he or she should report to Harry Krueper directly.

Finances at Krueper Engineering

By 1987 Krueper Engineering had seven main sources of revenues. Revenues show a constant upward trend, except for the year of 1980. Because Krueper Engineering sells a service, the firm has also developed a standard rate schedule.

The net income for 1987 was $219,068 on total sales of $1,781,701, for a net profit of 12.3 percent. The firm is essentially debt free; Krueper Engineering owns the 2-story building where it is located.

Computerization at Krueper

Accident computerization is a major concern faced by Harry Krueper as he testifies in court. Drawings done on the computer have become increasingly important, and attorneys expect Harry Krueper to be knowledgeable in this area.

Bookkeeping has already been computerized by the use of PCs, which are networked together. The other half of the firm, engineering, has its own network system which is 80% complete. Computerizing Krueper Engineering has taken longer than expected. The firm spent over $70,000 in 1987 for computers, and the firm decided to do its own customized programs. Some wonder how much longer it will take to finish the job. Paul Toomey, who spearheaded the computerization, wonders if the firm could have approached the computerization project in a different manner. Harry Krueper wonders: how much of the work should be done by the computer? He expressed much less faith in the computer than some others in the firm. "I have much more faith in people," he added. It is a continual test for him to see which is the more dependable and more accurate: people or the computer.

Krueper Engineering stores its case files on floppy disks. One employee noted that if a fire were to destroy the building, the firm would not have the means of reconstructing their records.

Planning at Krueper

Staff and the board of directors develop the policies and procedures for the firm through meetings which are fairly spontaneous. Because all board members are also employees, Harry Krueper will just call those individuals into his office if a major decision needs to be made. Staff meetings are usually held twice a month, and may last 1 to 2 hours. Discussions focus on office activities, new ideas, personnel or operations problems. Lately, discussions have focused on the implementation of the computer system.

Sitting on the current board of directors are Harry Krueper, Carson Storer, Fred Babbitt, John Toomey, Paul Toomey and Jim Hamlin, all insiders. Board meetings are short. Members do not get involved in setting objectives or goals. The idea of having an outsider member has not yet been considered. Occasionally though, an accountant or an attorney will attend a board meeting in an advisory capacity.

Physical Resources

Krueper Engineering is located on the entire second floor of a small two-story office building in San Bernardino, California. It has also four offices on the first floor of the same building. Remodeled in 1986, the Krueper Engineering suite is organized according to its six departments. Clerical functions appear off the left-hand corridor and technical functions off the right-hand side from the reception area.

In the middle between the two long passageways are conference rooms where staff can meet with customers. Three short hallways connect these two corridors. In these hallways are closets containing technical manuals used for more day-to-day operations. At the back of the suite is a large combination library-conference room with an adjoining outside deck with patio chairs. The patio overlooks a parking lot in San Bernardino.

All the offices have light blue walls and blue carpeting. Most people have either plants or pictures or both. There is also an assortment of drafting tables, computers and specialized equipment. Picture collages of the employees from various picnics and golfing events hang on the walls of reception area and the corridors. Harry Krueper stated he wants the atmosphere to seem "informal."

Harry Krueper expressed no problems with the firm's physical ability to expand. When the opportunity presented itself in 1974, Harry Krueper bought the building. The downstairs area of his building houses the offices of various community organizations. These include the League of Women Voters, San Bernardino Police Officers' Association, Legal Specialists of Smith & Peckben, U.S. Railroad Retirement Board, the Sierra Club and a local driving school.

Future of Krueper Engineering

One recurring concern shared by the employees is the issue of the firm's future without Harry Krueper. Since the firm has been unable to train a suitable successor, the loss of Harry Krueper would deprive the accident reconstruction team of their only expert witness. Some fear the pressure of constant and excessive workload may eventually lead to Harry Krueper's retirement. The employees do not want the firm to cease operation in his absence. Although it is not a widely known fact within the company, Harry Krueper does carry "key man" insurance.

Harry Krueper has also been described as a perfectionist and to date his standards are so exacting that a successor has not yet been trained. Yet Harry Krueper expressed he would like to have sixty people in the company within three years. He also hopes to have others do courtroom testifying, and he would like to hire an administrative manager within the next year. He would like to get more into research and be able to offer seminars in traffic accident investigation.

"I never thought we would be as large as we are. We have 44 people now. I set a goal not to go over about 30, but the needs of the engineering field are constantly expanding so you have to expand with them or you are lost. So you have to grow, but in a controlled manner...it's a lot different handling five people than 15. The ability to get someone under you to assist you to break this pyramid [is important]...I am now desperately looking for someone else to do [courtroom testifying] with me but very few want that kind of stress of going into court and fighting with the attorneys...There are people here who will do it but I don't want to force anybody into doing it...They would rather not get into that controversial area...but I do take staff people with me to court."

Harry Krueper wonders, "What is be the best way to proceed? Should he try to promote someone to be an administrative manager? Should he ask Carson Storer to do this? If he does get into presenting seminars, how often and how many should he give? He hasn't raised his rates in three years, should he do it now? How can he best protect his computer system? Should he store some records off-site? If yes, which ones? Finally, all of his people seem to be technicians. How can he develop them as managers? Who should be on his management team?

EXERCISE

1. What are the strengths of Krueper Engineering? Why is Krueper Engineering successful?

2. If the firm experiences a constant back-log of work in accident reconstruction, should they consider raising their prices to temper demand? If not, how are they going to handle the constant job stress in accident reconstruction?

3. What is the future of Krueper Engineering? Can Krueper Engineering survive without Harry Krueper?

4. How can Krueper Engineering plan for the future? What steps could they take now to prepare for the future?

5. Why is computerization an issue for small firms? What steps could other small firms take if they were to computerize?

CASE 13
LEWIS FOODS FLEET MANAGEMENT (B)[1]

On June 1, Lee Foods, an Omaha based distributor of cheese and other foodstuffs, acquired Wisconsin Food Distributors, a similar company also based in Omaha, Nebraska, to form Lewis Foods. Lee Foods distributed cheese and other foodstuffs to fast food restaurants, pizzerias and Mexican restaurants throughout the states west of the Mississippi River. Lee Foods owned a fleet of 160 tractors and 230 refrigerated trailers. Wisconsin Foods was a distributor of perishables to retail grocery stores in a nine state area centered in Omaha. Wisconsin Food Distributors had 90 tractors and 160 refrigerated trailers. A total of 26.5 million miles was driven by the two fleets in 1988 and that figure is remaining constant this year. Management anticipated that a total of 31.5 million miles, an additional 5 million miles, will be driven next year to support new customers.

At Lee Foods, John Richards, the chief mechanic, had also been serving as the dispatcher/fleet supervisor for the past year. At Wisconsin Foods, Al Lopez was the chief dispatcher with responsibilities similar to John's. After talking to both Al and John, Harlan Highsmith, the President of Lewis Foods, had the uneasy feeling that in the excitement generated by the potential savings in overhead costs, the increased productivity and efficiency due to economies of scale, and the larger market area, upper management may have overlooked some major issues in the merger of the two fleets.

---

[1] This case was written by Carl R. Ruthstrom, University of Houston-Downtown, David Cross, Robert Bosch Power Tool Corp., and Arthur Nelson, Lufkin Industries. Published with the permission of the North American Case Research Association.

As a result, he created the position of fleet manager to oversee the entire fleet. John Richards was to be named chief mechanic for Lewis Foods, the newly formed company and Al Lopez was to take the position of chief dispatcher when the merger of the two fleets was completed. Harlan Highsmith knew whom he wanted as fleet manager. He contacted Bill Carnes and offered him the job. He voiced his uneasy feelings and emphasized that he wanted a smooth changeover.

On July 15th, Bill Carnes became the Fleet Manager for Lewis Foods, the newly formed company. His first concern was to merge the operation and management of the two groups of trucks into a single fleet rather than continue to operate two separate fleets. The warehouse division of the company had completed their plans and expected to close the Wisconsin Foods facility in about 90 days. At that time all route planning and dispatching of loads would be out of the main warehouse.

Bill began his job of integrating the two groups into a single unit by evaluating the past performance of the two fleets. The major expenditures in fleet operations are for fuel, engine maintenance and tires. The staff anticipated Bill's information needs and prepared a report on fuel economy, maintenance and tire life for the trucking industry as shown in Table I and a comparison of the two fleets as shown in Table II. This report failed to identify the strengths and weaknesses of the operations of the two fleets. Bill Carnes visited both terminals and obtained the following additional information.

At Lee Foods, John Richards, the chief mechanic provided much of the information Bill wanted. The Lee fleet consists of tandem Kenworth and Peterbilt tractors. Eighty percent of the tractors are powered by the Cummins 350 Big Cam III governed at 1800 RPM. The phrase "governed at 1800 RPM" means that a governor or speed control device is installed on the engine to limit the maximum engine speed to 1800 revolutions per minute. This extends the operating life of the engines. The other twenty percent of the fleet's engine are Caterpillar 3406Bs governed at 1600 RPM.

The Lee fleet uses eight Goodyear 167 radial tires, four on each of the two drive axles, and two Goodyear Unisteel IIs on the single steering axle of each tractor. The trailers have another eight tires, four on each of the two axles. Tires removed from the steering axles are recapped and used on trailers. At the third recap, drive axle tires are moved back to the trailers. Only recapped tires are used on the trailers.

Two years ago, Lee had improved the fuel economy to 5 miles per gallon (MPG) by using fuel saving devices such as Paccar's Varashield air deflectors, Rudkin Wiley cab extenders, Rockford viscous fans, and lower horsepower engines. "But, somehow we seem to have hit a plateau and cannot get above 5 MPG," said John Richards.

TABLE I. Operating Performance-Industry Averages

Fuel Economy	5.7 mpg
Engine Overhauls	Every 450,000 miles to 475,000 miles
Tire Life	Recapped at every 150,000 miles, replaced at 500,000 miles

TABLE II. Lee/Wisconsin Performance Comparisons

	Lee Averages	Wisconsin Averages
Fuel Economy	5.0 mpg	5.8 mpg
Engine Overhauls	330,000 miles	450,000 miles
Tire Life	Recapped at every 100,000 miles, replaced at 345,000 miles	Recapped at every 150,000 miles, replaced at 500,000 miles

Driver comfort and safety have always been important considerations at Lee Foods as shown by the cabs with their deluxe carpeted interiors, AM/FM radio-tape players, air conditioning and seats with air-ride suspensions. The estimated cost of upgrading the interiors is $2000 per tractor. In addition, Lee has awarded drivers completing one million miles of safe driving with a $1000 bonus check. Every month, each driver attends a half-day driver safety and improvement class conducted by company instructors. As a result, Lee, with a turnover rate of three percent, has one of the lowest driver turnover rates in the trucking industry.

John Richards said, "There are not any labor problems at Lee. The only new drivers we have hired replaced those lost to retirement or physical disability."

At the Wisconsin Foods terminal, Al Lopez, the chief dispatcher, provided similar information. The Wisconsin fleet is entirely Kenworth tractors powered by the Cummins 350 Big Cam III engines governed at 1800 RPM. Fuel saving devices similar to those used by Lee are installed on all the tractors. Drivers are allowed to customize their tractors at their own expense resulting in interiors similar to the Lee tractors.

Two and one-half years ago, Wisconsin implemented a transportation improvement (TRIM) program. The program includes Stemco's on-board computer monitoring system (trip recorder) and Stemco's vehicle management system (VMS) software package. The recorders are installed in all Wisconsin's tractors. The hardware for this system averages $2200 per tractor. The memory cartridges are in the tractors when drivers are dispatched. At the end of a trip, the last thing a driver does is to remove the cartridge and turn it into dispatch. There he is given a blank cartridge, which he installs before leaving for the day. The driver enters his identification, the vehicle number and the route number at the start of each trip. In addition, he enters the number of gallons of fuel purchased for the trip. The computerized recorder stores times, engine RPM, speed in MPH, foot brake applications, and stops.

The data for each trip is downloaded from the memory cartridge to an IBM PC and subsequently stored on a floppy disc. The VMS program analyzes the data and prints out a Basic Trip Summary. Included in this summary are the statistics of various performance criteria management selected to evaluate driver performance, such as engine on time, idle time, road time, speed, RPM, and fuel consumption plus a grade (from 0 to 100) of the driver's performance.

The drivers were introduced to the TRIM program in meetings of 10 to 15 drivers. In these meetings, the emphasis was on improving fleet performance by identifying the problem areas in each driver's performance. Initially, the computer trip summaries showed 50% to 60% of the drivers were speeding (running above 58 MPH).

Al Lopez said, "We knew that the greatest savings for large tractors can be achieved through improved gas mileage and reduced wear on the vehicle. Better efficiency in either area would make a very visible difference in costs. We started informally counseling the drivers with emphasis on driver awareness of economical driving habits. The non-threatening approach produced dramatic results in reducing our fleet costs. Our fuel economy rose rapidly to 5.8 MPG where it remains today. Tire wear and engine maintenance costs have declined noticeably."

The single most noteworthy incident occurred when one of the drivers blew a Cummins engine in Texas. Cummins claimed it was attributable to over-revving and speed. The driver brought the memory cartridge with him when he flew back to Omaha. The VMS program analyzed the data and showed no speeding or over-revving saving the company a $17,000 engine repair bill.

"The most disappointing thing about the TRIM program is that we have never reached the anticipated 6-7 MPG that the Stemco salesmen assured us could be attained. In addition, we seem to be continually training new drivers on the system. Over 40% of our drivers have less than one year with the company," volunteered Al Lopez.

Further discussion with Al Lopez revealed that while 20 to 25% turnover of drivers was not unusual in the trucking industry, other underlying problems did exist. Both the chief dispatcher and the drivers feel that all the benefits of the computerized vehicle management system are reserved for the company.

The drivers are of the opinion that having "a cop" in the cab limits their potential earnings and does not allow the driver much freedom in terms of length of driving day, breaks, and sleeping time. Therefore, most of the turnover of drivers is generated by the lure of higher incomes and more individual freedom in other trucking companies.

Upon his return to his office, Bill Carnes decided to review the data in Tables I and II to compare the performance differences in fuel consumption, maintenance and tire wear. After reviewing the data in Table II, he decided to visit accounting and acquire cost data comparisons for the two fleets. Since the two fleets had continued operating separately, accounting had maintained separate books. The data Bill needed was readily available and Bill constructed the following table.

Table III. Lee/Wisconsin Cost Comparisons		
	Lee Averages	Wisconsin Averages
Cost per mile		
Equipment	$0.82	$0.65
Drivers	$0.61	$0.58
Miles per year		
Per tractor	112,708	94,075
Per driver	77,420	73,127

Before leaving, he questioned the accounting supervisor, Shirley Williams, about the differences in operating costs per mile between the two fleets. Shirley confirmed his finding that the Lee trucks were reporting higher fuel, tire and engine repair costs per truck than the Wisconsin fleet. Shirley Williams had begun investigating the differences in operating costs and found that both fleets were reporting approximately the same unit costs for fuel, tires, and engine overhauls as listed in Table IV. Shirley also found that the company policies for both fleets included the replacement of 15 percent of the fleet with new tractor-trailer rigs each year.

TABLE IV. Unit Costs

Item	Unit Price
Engine overhauls	$7000 per engine
Diesel fuel	$1.15 per gallon
New tires	
Steering Axles	$175 per tire
Drive Axles	$195 per tire
Recapping	$65 per tire

At first she was puzzled by the difference in the drivers' cost per mile. "Both groups of drivers are paid union scale. I'll have to look into this for you", Shirley said. As Shirley reviewed the records used to calculate the drivers' cost per mile for the two fleets, the only differences she could find were the safe driving bonuses paid to Lee drivers and lower pay to Wisconsin drivers during their initial probationary period. Shirley did find that the total pay and benefits package was larger for the Lee drivers because of the greater number of miles driven annually.

As Bill Carnes walked back to his office, he remembered Al Lopez's final remark, "Over 40% of our drivers have less than one year with the company." He made a mental note to confirm this with Shirley Williams in the morning.

When Bill Carnes returned to his office at 4:00 p.m., his secretary handed him a message to call Harlan Highsmith, President of Lewis Foods, immediately. Bill was surprised when Harlan Highsmith answered the phone without the assistance of a secretary.

After preliminary salutations, Harlan Highsmith said, "Bill, you have been with the company long enough to evaluate our current fleet operations. I've scheduled you to present your plans for integrating the Lee and Wisconsin fleet operations into a single fleet for 3:00 p.m., tomorrow. Have a good evening."

Bill Carnes realized that his recommended program must address both fleet operating costs and employee relations. He realized that capital investments may be needed in both fleets to achieve improvements in these areas.

At 6:00 p.m., before leaving the office, he called both John Richards and Al Lopez at home. He explained why he was calling and solicited their help in preparing for the 3:00 p.m. meeting. Both men agreed to be in Bill Carnes' office at 9:00 a.m. the next morning to assist in developing the plans for integrating the two fleets.

At 9:00 a.m., the next morning John Richards and Al Lopez report to Bill Carnes' office. By this time, Bill Carnes has begun to feel the same uneasiness that Harlan Highsmith, the President, had expressed when he hired Bill.

Bill Carnes begins, "After tossing and turning all night, I finally got dressed and prepared this list of questions that need to be answered."

1. What problems do you anticipate from the employees related to the merging of the two fleets if we do not make any changes in the treatment of the two groups of drivers?

2. What issues do you anticipate will cause the most concern among the drivers and what approach should we use to integrate the two fleets without alienating drivers?

3. Some of the drivers already qualify for the safe driving bonus. Could we continue this and add a bonus of $.03 per mile for every mile driven under 58 MPH?

4. Since any changes or improvements will cost money, where will we get the money to implement our plans?

5. Assuming that we decide to upgrade the tractors, would your first action be to install the Stemco trip recorders in all the Lee tractors or upgrade the driver comfort items in the Wisconsin tractors? Why?

"I have been listening to all of the drivers' comments at Lee and can give you a long list of answers for those first two questions," exclaimed John Richards.

"I'll bet my list of gripes is longer," said Al Lopez.

"Great! John, if you and Al will work on the first two questions, I'll get to work on the last three. Remember that we need more than just a list of gripes. we need a plan detailing how we are going to integrate the two groups of drivers without creating more problems. Let's meet back here at 11:00 a.m. and see what progress we have made."

EXERCISE

From a systems management viewpoint complete the following:

1.   Assist Bill Carnes by developing answers to the five questions listed above.

2.   In order for the Transportation Improvement Program to provide accurate analysis, data security must not be compromised. Develop your plans for insuring that the data files are not changed or deleted by unauthorized individuals.

3.   Since each trip file contains information about a specific driver's performance, what procedures would you implement to insure that the privacy of information rights of the drivers are not violated? How should these procedures be implemented?

CASE 14
LUFKIN-CONROE TELEPHONE EXCHANGE, INC.[1]

The Lufkin-Conroe Telephone Exchange, Inc. (LCTX), incorporated in 1986, is an independent local telephone exchange operating as a privately held public utility with administrative and operating offices located in Lufkin, Texas. Customers are located in Lufkin and its surrounding areas, in Alto (30 miles away), and in Conroe (approximately 85 miles south of Lufkin). The company serves approximately 66,000 access lines and is located in the Houston Local Access Transport Area (LATA). The service area extends over 1400 square miles and includes a network of nearly 4,000 miles of telephone cable.

The company employs over 400 people with 28 working in the Information Systems Department. The department has 19 programmers, three operators, and six people in administration and technical support. The computers and Information Systems staff are located in Lufkin. The computers discussed in this paper are used for company operations and commercial business. These are not the computers used by LCTX to record telephone call data. The latter, Northern Telecom digital switches, are located separately from the application computers with the only communication being via magnetic tape.

LCTX provides operator services for the Lufkin area and Southwestern Bell provides operator services for the Conroe customers. Typical user applications include billing inquiries from customers who call LCTX with billing questions and the accounting department staff making inquiries regarding accounts payable issues. One of the

---

[1]   This case was written by Charlene A. Dykman and Carl R. Ruthstrom, University of Houston-Downtown, and Chris B. Copenhaver, Lufkin-Conroe Telephone Exchange, Inc.

major systems supported by the Information Systems Department is the Toll Processing System which records and processes the billable telephone traffic traveling throughout the Lufkin-Conroe Telephone Exchange network.

The Toll Processing System

The Toll Processing System processes records entering the system from three different points. The first is LCTX (Northern Telecom switches) recorded calls that are long distance, mobile traffic, or directory assistance calls. The second entry point is calls recorded outside of the LCTX service area yet billable by LCTX. Included are credit card, collect, and third party billing calls. The third point of entry is conference calls originating in the Lufkin area. These are recorded manually and entered through a CRT. Also included here are Centralized Ticket Investigation (CTI) rebills following customer initiated inquiries regarding billing irregularities.

The information comes into this system in hexadecimal and is converted to character format. Calls not billed individually are separated out as are Access Usage Records. The latter are used to apportion out the monies to various companies whose facilities may have been used for the calls. The information goes through a rating process that involves a search of tables for the correct rate given the start time of the call, the call date, etc. Service charges for activities such as operator assistance are added at that time. The system then goes through a settlement process using industry guidelines and the Access Usage Records to set the actual value of the money to be shared between the phone companies.

Following this processing, a sampling process is conducted resulting in 5% of LCTX's traffic being sent by tape to Southwestern Bell each week. This is then sent to AT&T where the information is used for trend analysis. A third process divides out LCTX, Southwestern Bell, and Contel traffic. LCTX records some of Contel's traffic in one area. A tape containing this information is sent to Southwestern Bell and Contel each week.

LCTX uses different billing cycles to spread out the printing and mailing work load. Customers' billing cycles are determined by the first three digits of the phone number. There are two cycles for the Conroe area and three for the Lufkin area. This printing and mailing process occupies one full-time person. It is easy to see the heavy processing requirements that result from the complexity of today's telecommunication networks.

The Technology

LCTX processed all applications and development work on a single IBM System 38 until 1986. The Conroe and Alto areas were connected to the computer via modems and Lufkin was direct wired. Conroe users began to experience unacceptable response time as business grew dramatically during the 1980s. This was accompanied by growth in the size of the programming staff and the amount of development work being performed. A second System 38 was installed in October, 1986 and was dedicated to the Conroe users. Lufkin and Alto users, as well as the programming staff, used the larger of the two System 38s.

In July, 1988, IBM announced the introduction of the AS/400 line of computers. This line was to replace the System 38 in the IBM midrange family line and was to be much faster, more reliable, and have more memory than the System 38. The System 38 would no longer be manufactured by IBM and at some point in the future IBM would no longer offer service for the System 38. The 38 model would become what is known as "orphaned" and users would need to rely on private vendors for support and service.

IBM's long range plans for the AS/400 include increasing the potential of the computer over the next decade. This will be accomplished by new operating systems with minor changes to the hardware. When IBM announced the phase-out of the System 38, LCTX had to make several critical decisions about the future of the computer hardware they were using. LCTX was totally dependent on these computers and the enormous amounts of code, written in RPG3, which resides on these computers.

Alternatives

LCTX Information Systems personnel were now faced with alternatives to consider. What about making no changes? This would not require any capital investments or hardware or software changes. However, over time, support for the 38s would become a major issue and this prevented serious consideration of the "do nothing" alternative.

The second option was to purchase two AS/400 computers and configure them in the same manner as the 38s with a small one dedicated to Conroe users and a larger one for Lufkin and Alto users and developmental activities. This offered possibilities for one computer serving as a backup for the other, avoided problems with user competition for batch processing resources, assured good response time for Conroe users, gave flexibility to the operations staff for scheduling the nightly production jobs, and gave the programming staff easy access to test data on the same machine. This configuration had some disadvantages also. Production jobs requiring data from both machines meant operator intervention and tape handling. Program changes had to be installed on two machines and complex interfaces were needed for access to common applications that shared data because these applications resided on one machine. Redundant programs and data existed and this required more memory. With programmers doing testing on a production machine, there was always vulnerability to erroneous updates of production data.

The third alternative considered was to purchase two AS/400s and configure one as a developmental platform and the larger one to serve the entire user population. This would eliminate complex hardware interfaces, separate development work from the production data, reduce memory requirements caused by program and data redundancy, and eliminate the competition for resources between the users and the programming staff. There were disadvantages associated with this configuration also. Program testing now would require the importing of live data to the development machine. Nightly production scheduling would become much more difficult and the volume of production jobs on one machine would nearly double. Jobs that shared data could no longer be run at the same time. Response time for the users in Lufkin, who access the system through modems, might degrade during peak periods.

The manager of Information Systems at LCTX has to make a decision that will have a long-term impact on the department, the entire company, and its users. Neither of the viable alternatives is without risks. The manager contemplates the future, weighing the various advantages and disadvantages, and finally develops a proposal and recommendation for the acquisition and implementation of the AS/400 computers.

EXERCISE

1.   What are the most important issues to be considered in this decision?

2.   Which of the alternatives would you recommend? Why?

3.   What about the future? How can Information Systems management assure that this decision will be a viable one for a reasonable period of time.

4.   What are the unique aspects of this particular business, a small-town telephone exchange, that affect decisions being made in the Information Systems Department? What impact do these unique aspects have on the department?

5.   What other alternatives do you think should have been given consideration in this case? What are their advantages and disadvantages?

CASE 15
NEW ENGLAND TELEPHONE[1]

Paul O'Brien, Executive Vice President, New England Telephone, was going to a luncheon meeting with his executive counterpart at AT&T. He was mulling over the previous day's discussion which would likely be today's luncheon topic. Two key executives had brought to his attention an AT&T letter to New England Telephone requesting action needed to shorten the length of time for installing the various types of special service communication lines. Six months had elapsed, and New England Telephone had made no response to AT&T's request.

O'Brien knew that this had been a problem for some time. High demand levels and new technologies, coupled with the more competitive environment of deregulation, presented a challenge New England Telephone just had not been able to meet. In fact, at one point standard installation times had been increased in order to reduce the backlog.

Returning from lunch a short time later, one thing was clear: New England Telephone would have to reduce its installation times or the utility's relationships with customers and future operations would be jeopardized. AT&T could choose to use new technologies to bypass New England Telephone and go directly to its long distance customers. Alternatively, AT&T could reach its long distance customers through telephone lines provided by new, unregulated companies offering shorter installation times. Compounding the problem, it was not a viable alternative to reduce

[1] This case was written by Karen D. Loch, Georgia State University, Patricia McDougall, Georgia Institute of Technology, and Karl G. Hellman, Hellman & Loch, based on input from John Sargent, New England Telephone.

117

installation times for only AT&T and other carriers, without reducing installation times for all other customers at the same time. These customers had the option to switch from New England Telephone to either AT&T or the new unregulated companies for the local component of their special service lines.

New England Telephone needed to transform itself from a regulated monopoly mindset that could set its own installation times to a competitive mindset with installation times driven by customer needs. This transformation would give New England Telephone a chance to reposition itself on the competitively critical dimension of installation times. Repositioning would take away a potential source of advantage from AT&T and an existing source from the new entrants.

Resolute in his action, O'Brien asked Jim Wooster, the executive in charge of relationships with the interexchange carriers (AT&T, MCI, and Sprint) to spearhead a task force to reduce installation times. Jim appointed John Sargent, a veteran operations executive, as task force leader.

Divestiture and Deregulation

Prior to divestiture and competition, the Bell System provided telephone and related services end-to-end. Individual customers were unable to exert much leverage for improved service. Installation times were not a significant problem to New England Telephone. One executive reflected on the prevailing attitude at the time:

> Everyone had the feeling that the customer would prefer shorter installation times and we felt there must be some way to shorten them, but it was not a major priority.

Divestiture and deregulation signaled a competitive free-for-all and opened new opportunities for entrepreneurial start-ups. In the changed market structure, local telephone companies were poised for entry and long distance carriers butted heads in competition. Technology exploded in the highly competitive telephone equipment business. The precise effect of breaking up the Bell System was impossible to gauge; not since the break-up of Standard Oil in 1911 had the government initiated such an action.

Local Bell Operating Companies (BOCs), providing service under their pre-divestiture, more familiar names, were consolidated into seven regional holding companies (RHCs). New England Telephone and New York Telephone were made part of the NYNEX regional holding company.

Interexchange carriers such as AT&T, MCI, and Sprint became middle players in the process. While individual customers purchased one, two or even twenty special service lines, interexchange carriers were purchasing thousands. As one executive explained,

> Instead of having a lot of little customers who might or might not band together and express their dissatisfaction, there were several huge customers who suddenly had leverage.

Competitive Repositioning - Customer Service Orientation

Divestiture and deregulation wrought massive changes and the need for competitive repositioning by New England Telephone. New England Telephone executives, however, are quick to point out that it is unfair to describe the company as not being customer service oriented prior to deregulation. One executive proudly recalled a picture set in rural New England of a telephone craftsman skiing in a blizzard to fix a downed cable. For years, the Bell companies used the picture to exemplify the attitude of service and dedication telephone workers felt.

New England Telephone had to change its definition of customer service. No longer could service be according to New England Telephone's ground rules. Today, company executives state, "service is according to the market and customers' standards."

The Customer

Why had it taken New England Telephone so long to respond to AT&T, other carriers, and all other customers? The answer lies in the new complexities of the relationships that occurred with divestiture of the old Bell System. Suddenly, interexchange companies became suppliers and customers with viable alternatives to New England Telephone services. New England Telephone had to resolve this new challenge in order to address its internal service problems.

An internal crusade that started with presentations to the board of directors, and was reinforced in company publications and at team meetings, successfully illustrated the importance of these customers to New England Telephone. AT&T and the other carriers represented the largest single market for the company's revenues.

Employees came to realize that a substantial slice of every paycheck dollar was contributed by the interexchange carriers. They understood that only by providing more responsive, high quality service could New England Telephone prevent carriers from considering some degree of by-passing the local company's network. This threat was underscored by the success of Teleport, a post-divestiture entrant who was able to offer shorter installation times. Teleport had already succeeded in making an impact in the New York City market at the expense of New England Telephone's sister company, New York Telephone. Teleport had announced plans to enter the Boston market next. A whole new customer focus was in order. One executive said:

> What we needed was thorough understanding by the employees that we wanted the carriers in our territory to become highly successful in New England, through us, not despite us. We wanted our employees thinking of AT&T and the other carriers as our largest, most valuable customers.

Service Strategy

Competing in the deregulated environment required that New England Telephone reconsider its service strategy. Under regulatory protection, telephone companies were required only to maintain satisfaction levels above certain thresholds. Deregulation, combined with technological innovations, virtually demolished entry barriers and market boundaries. It was imperative that New England Telephone offer superior service because it was not the low cost producer. Failure to provide superior service would mean a risk of losing significant revenues to the competition. In 1987 alone, Regional Bell Operating Companies lost over $2.2 billion to bypass (a process by which customers use microwave technology and other carriers to bypass the local telephone company). Now, to be competitive, New England Telephone needed to become the premier service provider in their customers' view.

The People

Two themes emerged as keys to transforming the organization's customer service strategy for all employees:

1. To live and breathe service and quality.

2. To understand that the proper measure of service and quality is what the market place and customer thinks, not what the employee thinks.

Ironically, in an industry exploding with technology, it was mainly people that reduced time frames. An interdepartmental task force has received unanimous credit within New England Telephone for successfully reducing installation times.

The task force's charter was to reduce the time to install special lines not normally provided to residences or small businesses; 1) voice grade, 2) designed WATS (wide area telephone service), and 3) digital data services.

This task force was not the first to address the reduction of installation times. In fact, earlier task forces had presented similar recommendations, which were never implemented. Why was this task force successful, where others had failed? What was different about the management of this task force and the people on it? The three steps highlighted in the following discussion -- (1) forming the task force, (2) creating the proper environment, and 3) solving the problem -- could be applied to other organizations using task forces to address a range of problems.

Forming the Task Force

First, the creation of this task force was different -- it was executively mandated and told, "we are not going to debate whether, we are going to determine how." Only when the situation had become a high level corporate concern did it become a "corporate priority." From the very beginning, the task force had top level commitment, a clear mission, and a time line of sixty days.

The representatives chosen for the successful task force were hand-picked by their department heads and vested with the authority to act for the entire department. This requirement had the effect of getting senior members who could make a difference. Previous task force recommendations had not been implemented, whereas the membership of this task force represented the very individuals within the organization who were charged with implementation.

Representatives from every department involved in the special services installation process were assigned to the task force. Thus, the entire spectrum of the process was incorporated, creating an interdepartmental task force, in contrast to previous task forces which included only some of the involved departments. The fragmented nature of previous task forces contributed to their failures by not addressing the entire chain of the installation process.

The people appointed to the task force were described as being both technically competent experts in their own areas, as well as having a good working knowledge of the other departments' operations. It was important that members could converse readily with other members, and that they could not be bluffed by anyone else. One member explained:

A member may be competent in their own field, but have no idea of what happens in the adjoining operations. That person tends to become very protective of his own operation. But if task force members have a general knowledge and someone says it takes me three days to get the order through my department, the other members have an idea of what that operation entails and can refute the statement, or they can probe with questions and make suggestions.

Creating the Proper Environment

The sixty day time line fueled the sense of urgency surrounding the task force and contributed to gaining the full time commitment required of each member. One industry observer contrasted this task force with a typical task force in a consensus management environment:

> It is not unusual for management to serve on multiple task forces at the same time. Their membership requires little more than their presence to keep their department informed of decisions. In fact, because of the sheer time demands and the limited need for decision making, it becomes standard practice for managers to send subordinates to substitute for them in meetings. Task forces can be permanent, or near permanent, meeting monthly for years.

In the beginning, the task force met daily accelerating the breaking down of departmental barriers and created a spirit of cooperation, teamwork, and trust. But, perhaps more important was the philosophy adopted by the group that customer needs were number one. One member felt that this was what made the task force work:

> We set the customer needs as number one, far and away above departmental needs. . . . perceived that all departments were fair game for change . . . People were there for the company and the customer. It took a while, but once the team was working together for a week or two some of the departmental barriers began to drop.

Creating an atmosphere of cooperation and honesty can probably be credited to John Sargent's leadership of the group. The chairman's early ground rules and systematic approach to problem-solving were critical. No minutes were taken at the meetings. This allowed the group to more openly discuss reasons reduction of installation times had been unsuccessful in the past. As trust grew, more dirty linen was aired, but without the risk of gee whiz stories of what you always suspected but never knew for sure happened in another department. Debates stayed within the task force. Petty grievances and parochialism died.

Solving the Problem

Expanding the customer concept, Sargent divided the installation process down to individual tasks at the departmental level with each hand-off representing a customer contract. There was the true customer -- the external one -- that gave the order. The front-line person then became, in effect, a service provider to the next department in the process. Each subsequent player in the process played first the role of internal customer and then changed hats to become service provider for the next department in line.

The concept was very successful because it built a bond between members in the team. This was a first step in recognizing that if the internal customers do not work together, the external ones suffer. In the past there had always existed a degree of competition between the departments. The company had fostered this competition through productivity and other internal measures which were budget driven and tied to the compensation reward system. An unhealthy internal competitive situation resulted such that the focus was departmental rather than process oriented.

The task force had to tear down the established walls between departments and define the underlying process for providing special services. In what had grown to be a somewhat defensive environment, departments had negotiated their own "mini standards" within the company's promised installation standards. They discussed possible changes in each department's operations or elimination of some tasks, viewing the installation as a continuous process where departments shared responsibility for outcomes.

Momentum began to build once intervals started to be reduced. People felt good about themselves, particularly knowing that the company and the customer recognized their efforts. A win-win situation was created.

Systems

Systems, both physical hardware and abstract procedural systems, played a key support role in reducing installation times. The task force began by defining the existing installation systems and procedures. They traced the flow of installation orders from the customer's first call to the printing of the bill. They identified the activities being performed, how long each took, where time was being lost, and roadblocks to streamlining and reducing total elapsed time.

Quality Saves Time

Poor quality was the major contributor to lengthy installation times. The task force member representing the first link in the process admits in horror that the quality of service orders at the beginning of the process had an error rate as high as 30 percent. Other departments had to compensate.

> Everybody had to live with poor quality up stream, and that's why we needed so much time in the process.

The task force focused on reducing errors. The service order work group increased its percentage of error free orders from 70 percent to 97.3 percent. They won the first award given by the Quality Institute, an internal organization which reports directly to the presidents of New England Telephone and NYNEX.

Four systems supported improvement in quality:

(1)   contracts between adjoining departments, specifying timeliness and quality levels;

(2)   timeliness and quality measurements;

(3)   a computerized system which tracked each order's progress through the process; and

(4)   feedback on performance.

Sargent introduced the concept that every employee is a service provider working for an internal customer, i.e. the next department in the order flow. Written contracts were negotiated between providers and internal customers that specified quality levels and the timing of hand-offs. Each department negotiated contracts both as a customer and as a service provider.

Sargent's motto was: "If you don't measure it, don't do it." He knew the tendency in large organizations was to declare victory and abandon the war, that is to say things have changed when they really have not. In addition to timeliness measurements, a quality measurement process was developed as an integral part of the tracking system. In the process, each department evaluated incoming orders and returned those that did not meet interdepartmental quality commitments.

The task force expanded the capabilities of an existing system, Trunk Integrated Record Keeping System (TIRKS), which was being used by some departments to track orders and measure timeliness. The task force extended system use to include every department in the process and, most significantly, to measure quality. The members used TIRKS to save time in three ways:

First, TIRKS provided status information on orders for all departments. This eliminated thousands of telephone calls each week between departments to check status.

Second, TIRKS gave the task force members the information they needed to focus on the problem and opportunities to reduce installation times. TIRKS information was posted on the wall for discussion, diagnosis of the cause of lost time, and solution development. A team spirit evolved as the task force members were committed to getting the whole job done. This focus on problem solving and the lack of finger pointing were keys to rapid progress. One member recalled his experience:

> If the roadblock happened to be in my department, they would try to help me. They would look at the numbers and see what the problem was.

Third, TIRKS reduced installation times through increased automation of the process. While the system was in place prior to the formation of the task force, it consisted of non-integrated modules. Manual intervention was required to take data from one system and reenter it into the next system. The TIRKS expert on the task force explained the savings gained from automation:

> Let's say a [manual bridge from one system to the next] took four days. Reducing errors might reduce the time needed by one day. If you eliminate it [the manual bridge], the whole four days just disappears.

At present, 30 percent of the orders go through TIRKS completely unaided by manual intervention. Goal for year-end 1989 is 50 percent.

Feedback

In the past, communication between departments was confrontational. Several members observed that they did not know each other before their appointment to the task force, suggesting a lack of communication between departments involved in the installation process.

The task force felt it was important to establish positive, cooperative communications. Here are some of the steps they took:

1.   The concept of being a service provider to an internal customer created positive contacts as commitments were negotiated and fulfilled. This

contact and focus on performance involved internal customers in other departments' problems, often leading them to take a personal interest in helping other departments meet their time and quality objectives.

2.   At critical times in the project, the task force used the "war room" to identify problems as they developed and to prevent them from escalating. This concept paid off, when unexpectedly, 100 orders came in from a carrier and the service center needed specific coaching on how to meet the surge with its new, untested procedures.

3.   Reports were provided by the TIRKS system and departments were trained in their use. A report based on quality commitments was developed and generated everyday and became one of the main quality management tools. Executive reports were provided only once a month. The time between top management reports gave departments the opportunity to respond to problems and correct them without top management pressure.

4.   The task force kept everyone informed about what they were trying to accomplish and their progress. Customers were notified as shorter intervals became available. New England Telephone's top management was briefed on changes and shown how to read and interpret the new reports. Meetings were held regularly with the departments involved in implementation. The task force was careful to position measurements as information, not punishment.

The Benefits of a Shorter Installation Time

Shorter installation times responded not only to New England Telephone's largest customer's complaints, but other customers also received faster service. As time frames improved, so did the quality of service. One task force member suggested that improved quality was a function of the shorter interval, explaining that there was less time for things to go wrong and for people to lose focus on the task. New England Telephone had been known for the longest installation times in the industry. The success of the task force in implementing reductions brought them to a competitive level.

Better service resulted in increased revenues. Providing quality service faster improved cash flow by generating revenues earlier. Personnel needs were reduced as less manual intervention was needed to correct quality deficiencies. A conservative estimate suggested increased revenues around $2 million for the first year. In summary, New England Telephone found it possible to not only reduce installation time frames, but improve quality, and do it cheaper at the same time.

Change Management

It is important to note that the task force represented the beginning rumblings of change that reached into the very depths of the organization. Change management became imperative in order for the interval reduction to be successful. A major effort was undertaken to create an understanding of the need for reduction without sacrificing on-time performance. This was achieved in two ways. First, team meetings, department periodicals, and bulletins were used to internally spread the word on installation reduction and get the ranks of non-management to buy-in.

Second, Sargent and the task force team members practiced stakeholder management with the managements of the affected departments. This was one of the keys since the management compensation plan was tied to percent on-time performance. Installation time standards were a sensitive topic, and management was naturally concerned about reduction when they were already having problems meeting the existing installation times. In order to make progress, the task force members had to negotiate a temporary "immunity" with management to protect bonuses while it worked to improve standards. Over time, as the respective departments found that they were in fact able to meet the shorter installation time frames, their fears subsided.

Future Challenges

New England Telephone and its experience with reducing installation times demonstrates a service-oriented, quality driven approach to competition. In the words of one of the utility's executives regarding future challenges:

> Service and quality are going to separate the winners from the losers in American Industry in the next five to ten years. It is driven by both local and foreign competition. Companies will have to live and breath quality and have to understand that the measure of quality and the measure of service is what the market place and the customer thinks.

A significant outgrowth of the task force has been a new consciousness to strive for quality. The driving force is quality as defined by the customer, a refined concept. The traditional customer still exists but the concept of an internal customer, the department downstream in the process, has also been institutionalized. The communication network that was established fostered teamwork that developed a sense of pride in doing something right and something for the betterment of the company, which in turn was better for the individual employee.

The members of the task force have changed since its inception but installation times continue to be reduced. Employees are included and offer suggestions. Infusing the philosophy of service and quality into the fabric of the corporation has strategically affected New England Telephone's new competitive position in the industry.

EXERCISE

1.   What are the major issues in this case and how do they relate to each other?

2.   Define the critical elements that made the task force a success. Why were these important?

3.   Discuss the installation process as a "system". How did this understanding manifest itself in the workings of the task force?

4.   Assume the role of the leader of the task force process. What are the instructions you would give to the group and how would you expect the group to function?

CASE 16
OFFICE AUTOMATION AT VACBAG[1]

On a bright morning in March of 1992, Nicholas (Nick) Case, Senior Systems Analyst for Vacbag, Incorporated, was reviewing the progress of the office automation project on which he had worked over the past eleven months. Although a change in top management had caused a company-wide reorganization that had delayed the project, it was now moving with full top management support. Also, the vendor selection process was well underway with four vendors vying to obtain the contract for hardware and software.

Case had spent considerable time studying actual case histories of how office automation had been introduced at other companies. This secondary information, along with primary information obtained during meetings with Vacbag's thirty-member office automation task force, had given Case invaluable guidance throughout the project. A cost/benefit analysis had shown that office automation could feasibly increase office productivity at Vacbag. In the back of Case's mind, however, there was a nagging question: How would the office personnel react to the new system?

Company Background

In 1958, the Consolidated Vacuum Company established a vacuum bag manufacturing division to control vacuum bag cost and quality. This division was originally named

---

[1] This case was prepared by J. D. Van Brink, Information Systems Consultant, Gary C. Pickett, Tennessee Technological University, and Michael L. Menefee, Pembroke State University.

the Maroa Vacuum Bag Company, since it was located in Maroa, Illinois, some 10 miles north of Decatur, Illinois (Consolidated's headquarters).

Maroa operations began with only two employees using sewing machines to make vacuum bags. Although its start was modest, the company grew rapidly and, in 1963, introduced the Vacbag brand. In 1966, this brand's success encouraged the company to rename the division Vacbag, Incorporated. That same year marked the manufacturing operation's move from the small Maroa building to its present location in Chattanooga, Tennessee. The data processing function was housed at this location and eventually became the company's management information systems department. Because of its central location, Kansas City, Missouri, was chosen in 1968 as the site for the company's marketing offices. Also in 1968, a small manufacturing facility was built in Beckley, West Virginia.

Today, Vacbag employs about 1,500 people worldwide and carries over 5,000 products. Vacbag's line of cleaning fluids, cloths, hoses, nozzles, and bags makes it the leader in heavy-duty vacuum accessory design, innovation, and manufacturing. Vacbag's vacuum bags are manufactured for a number of leading original equipment manufacturers.

A strong dedication to innovation and quality has been a major factor in Vacbag's success. This dedication has made Vacbag the trend setter in the marketplace with the largest engineering and laboratory group in the heavy-duty vacuum industry. Vacbag's innovations include an extraction method of vacuuming, the first pleated paper full-flow bag as standard on consolidated engines, and a non-toxic cleaner marketed under the name GCP. The company's MM-418 spin-on full-flow vacuum bag has had a profound effect on the heavy-duty industry since 1975. By 1978, over 90 percent of the spin-on full-flow bags in the marketplace had come from the Chattanooga plant.

Vacbag's filter quality standards were established by Consolidated, a company known for its dedication to quality. Although Vacbag's bags are used on Consolidated vacuums and manufactured to specifications established by Consolidated, Vacbag will make vacuum bags for other customers to meet their individual specifications.

Office Automation at Vacbag

Vacbag has used automated office equipment since July, 1976, when word processing equipment was installed at the Tennessee location. The Kansas City location started using word processing equipment in May, 1977. Vacbag has used on-line application software for order processing since May, 1980, and for their Manufacturing Production and Control System (MPACS) since September, 1981. Presently, Vacbag uses three

Apple IIs and eight IBM PCs for a variety of office work. The Chattanooga location houses a Sperry-Univac 1110/71 mainframe, and the Beckley location houses an IBM mainframe.

Vacbag's Office Automation Project

The office automation project at Vacbag was initiated by Vacbag's president in February of 1991. The goals of the project were for Vacbag to gain a competitive edge by:

1. handling information more efficiently and cost effectively.

2. arming managers to allow them to examine more alternatives and to make more informed decisions without costly staff work.

3. reducing overhead expenses through improved productivity.

The purpose/objective of the project was to develop an office automation master plan that would conform to the corporate goal of improving productivity by 30 percent from July 1991 to July 1992. Office productivity improvements would be measured by decreased overhead, including labor and supplies, as a percentage of total product costs.

The project scope would cover three main areas. First, emphasis would be placed on processing/communicating information and functions that involved a meaningful percentage of employees' total job functions. Second, the study would initially address Vacbag's United States operations and communications to and from the company's worldwide operations. Finally, the study would address all office functions in the organization from clerical and administrative to managerial and executive.

The Management Information Systems (MIS) group was assigned responsibility for preparing a tentative schedule of project activities. This schedule is presented in Exhibit 1. The first responsibility was to form an office automation task force. An office automation core team was formed, including ten key supervisors from various line and staff functions at Vacbag. Some core team members were volunteers who felt that their participation would benefit the automation study and keep them informed of the study's progress. By late July, 1991, this team had recruited other members to increase the task force to thirty members. The task force's role was to give direction and support to the project.

Exhibit 1
Office Automation Tentative Project Milestones

	Tentative Schedule
Assign responsibilities	March - April 1991
Prepare a questionnaire	March - April 1991
Identify our problems and needs	April - May 1991
Evaluate problems and needs	May 1991
Prioritize problems and needs	June 1991
Finalize OA strategy	June 1991
Evaluate hardware/software	July 1991
Make recommendations	August 1991
Start pilot installation	October 1991
Evaluate pilot installation	February 1992

The MIS group was responsible for coordinating task force efforts and meetings. Also, the MIS group prepared periodic reports that summarized and reviewed project progress and gave the task force valuable secondary information to consider.

By August, the MIS group and some key task force members had prepared a questionnaire to identify problems and needs in Vacbag's office systems. The questionnaire was widely distributed throughout all organizational levels and areas at Vacbag's Chattanooga, Beckley, and Kansas City locations. Interviews were used to supplement the questionnaires.

The task force analyzed the questionnaire and interview results and determined that office automation would definitely address and resolve several office problems at Vacbag. A list of these office problems appears in Exhibit 2. The task force speculated that there were several other office problems that office automation could possibly address and resolve. A list of these office problems appears in Exhibit 3. The task force also prepared a list of office problems that office automation would not address and resolve. The task force decided that these office problems would require corporate attention. A list of these office problems appears in Exhibit 4. The last five office problems in Exhibit 4 were those that the task force felt could possibly be addressed and resolved by office automation if they received appropriate corporate attention.

The task force considered several features of an office automation system that would enhance office productivity and communications. These features included electronic mail, filing, message-taking, spreadsheets, meeting and calendar scheduling, word processing, and computer graphics. The task force also desired a universal workstation system that would allow access to mainframe data bases and multi-computer access. Teleconferencing was a desired feature, but one that would be incorporated in the future.

Exhibit 2
Office Problems Definitely Addressed and
Resolved by Office Automation

Manual Calculation
Timeliness of Information
Slow main delivery between company locations (especially international)
Late distribution of engineering changes and releases
Manual reformatting of computer-generated data
Word processing turnaround time; retyping/changing documents
Too much paper shuffling
Reaching people by phone; access to WATS/tie line
Hardware compatibility (universal workstation)
Retrieving documents from files
Insufficient CRT/micro access
Lack of communication between departments/locations
Finding people to get/share information
Lack of access to information when away from office
Receiving/distributing internal mail
Lack of ability to cross index memos
Getting copies made
Difficulty of scheduling meetings
Inability to locate regional managers on the road

In August 1991, Vacbag's president left the company. A reorganization followed wherein the MIS group retained its staff status but reported to the vice-president of administration instead of the vice-president controller.

In late August, Case was assigned to the project as the MIS liaison. Because of the company-wide reorganization, the project was delayed until Case was assigned as project manager in December 1991. Case put together a cost/benefit analysis from information gathered by the task force. Several office automation cost areas were considered, including hardware and peripherals, software, hardware connections, and

Exhibit 3
Office Problems Possibly Addressed and Resolved by Office Automation

Approval/decision process takes too long
Access to engineering data (especially quality control printouts)
Incomplete/inaccurate information
Cannot send CAMS/Telex any hour of the day
Access to computer-generated documents
Lack of knowledge of what information is available
Access to Consolidated's systems
Poor response time from Consolidated
Meetings too unstructured
High turnover of personnel
Some departments do not have clerical support
Items lost in the internal mail
Having to send follow-up memos
Memo formats too diverse

Exhibit 4
Problems Not Resolved by Office Automation that Require Corporate Attention

Reporting all data--not just exceptions
Hard to determine correct party to give/get information to/from
Top down information not shared on regular, timely basis
Too many meetings
Unscheduled meetings
Meetings too long
Second shift personnel don't have ready access to first shift personnel
Office environment not conducive to productivity (light, temperature, noise)
Guidelines/policies not spelled out/practiced
Short-term priority changing
Replanning too often
Management reporting too detailed
Bureaucratic procedures
Approval/decision process takes too long
Lack of communication between departments/locations
Meetings too unstructured
High turnover of personnel
Insufficient time to learn new tools

training. A list of these automation cost areas appears in Exhibit 5. The analysis also presents several savings areas that office automation could enhance by supporting better managerial planning for future office needs. A list of these automation savings areas appears in Exhibit 6. The task force concluded that office automation would positively increase office productivity.

Exhibit 5
Office Automation Cost Areas

CPUs, disk drives, and tape drives	Connection in Decatur (IBMs)
Software	Connection to Beckley (IBMs)
CRTs and printers	Training of computer operations
Cabling (CRTs to CPUs; CPU to CPU)	Training of users
Modems and muxes	System administrators (4)
Data grade phone lines	Workstation upgrades - furniture
Computer room upgrades	Vendor office system support

Exhibit 6
Office Automation Savings Areas

Planned future CRT additions
Planned future communication equipment additions
Planned or unplanned microcomputer additions
Planned microcomputer modem additions
Planned microcomputer software additions (spreadsheet, graphics, word processing)
Planned future data line additions/upgrades
Planned workstation upgrades (furniture)
Planned telecommunications upgrade

Training was a specific office automation cost area that raised several questions for the task force to consider. Since training would be an integral part of implementing office automation, answers to these questions were needed initially. The task force considered who would require training, where the training would take place, and who would be responsible for the training. Some of those questions include:

o   How many system administrators?

o   Will we set up training rooms?

o   Will training be part of corporate training, information
       center, totally separate, or a combination?

o   How will the training be broken down (how much manda-
       tory vs. choice)?

o   Will each area have its local expert (as in MPACS)?

o   How much training will be handled internally vs. vendor supplied?

The vendor selection process began in January 1992. Office automation hardware and
software from four computer vendors were selected for review based upon a
preliminary analysis of their capabilities, costs, and service. These vendors included
Data General Corporation, Digital Equipment Corporation, International Business
Machines, and Sperry-Univac, Inc. The task force planned to use four super
minicomputers with one computer in both Kansas City and Beckley, and two in
Chattanooga. In early March 1992, the task force felt that a vendor would be selected
by the end of the month.

Expectations

In March, while discussing the office automation project, Case mentioned:

> Until you do a detailed study of all the tasks to be done, you have no
> idea of the magnitude of the project. The biggest problems that I
> anticipate with the project down the road include financial backing,
> maintaining human resource support, and maintaining momentum to
> keep interest, especially regarding the task force.

> MIS will probably be the implementation leaders for the project. We
> will not be trainers or administrators, and we will not be primarily
> concerned with the day-to-day problems associated with office automa-
> tion. User administrators will probably be assigned to deal with the
> minor problems--two in Chattanooga, one in Kansas City, and one in
> Beckley.

> Existing personnel will have to be trained over time as we build up to
> where we want to be. After that point, all new hires will probably be
> trained to use automated office equipment before beginning to work.
> The more office skills they have coming on board, the better.

> I expect that a pilot project will be ready by January of 1993. It could
> be sooner if the data communication lines necessary for the pilot could
> be installed earlier, but there is a large backlog at AT&T.

One advantage that this project has going for it is the fact the Consolidated's president is in favor of office automation.

Case felt confident that office automation would result in many benefits for Vacbag. In the short term, office personnel would be more efficient and in better control of their various duties. Creating, processing, storing, distributing, and retrieving information would be improved considerably. Information would be more timely, relevant, accurate, and concise. Also, improved communications would enhance coordination of the manufacturing and marketing functions.

In the long term, improved communications would enhance the planning process at Vacbag. Office automation would help personnel at all levels to manage their resources better and to work toward company goals more effectively.

These improvements would give Vacbag a definite competitive edge and maintain its industry leadership. Top management from both Vacbag and Consolidated Vacuum expected Vacbag to grow steadily over the next five years, to provide more jobs and new challenges.

But Case wanted to exercise caution with optimism since he knew that the ultimate success or failure of the project rested, literally, in the users' hands. Case expected to be heavily involved with vendor selection, project implementation, and evaluation over the next six months. Case knew that he needed to anticipate how the users would react to the new system before it was implemented. Only then would Case and the task force be able to plan an office automation implementation strategy.

EXERCISE

1. What is the significance of top management support for the project? Does the re-organization have an impact on the OA project?

2. Discuss the company's goals for OA. Are they realistic? What other goals should be added to the list?

3. Is the company realistic in its assessment of what office automation can do with regard to productivity and competitive advantage?

4. Evaluate the composition of the task force. Identify advantages and disadvantages. Make recommendations with justifications.

5.   Are the project milestones reflected in Exhibit 1 sufficient for planning the project? Are the times realistic? What adjustments do you recommend?

6.   Design a questionnaire to be administered to the users of the new system to assess their attitudes toward the project and system. Keep in mind that the findings will influence your implementation strategy.

7.   What criteria should be used after implementation to measure the effectiveness of the system?

8.   Respond to the questions posed by the task force concerning training. Develop a training plan that will be presented to company management.

CASE 17
SOUTHERN UTILITY[1]

"Southern Utility" is a large investor owned electric utility serving 1.3 million custo-mers in a 5,000 square mile area. It is one of the ten largest utilities in the United States with a workforce of over 11,000 employees. Revenues typically exceed $3.5 billion annually.

Southern Utility uses telecommunications networking facilities for data communi-cations in support of an information systems processing environment supporting more than 2,500 online terminals. Based upon recommendations submitted by T. J. Parker, Chief Information Officer at Southern Utility, executive management recently approved a program that includes a provision for each professional employee of Southern Utility to have a terminal "on the desk" within four years.

These plans require the installation and support of 1800 more terminal devices on the network within the first year. The Information Systems Department needs an effective approach for managing network expansion. This methodology will be used to evaluate and control the sizing, sequencing, and timing of planned modifications to the network, and to control the levels of costs associated with those modifications. At Southern Utility the key to achieving an effective network management strategy is the development of a systematic methodology for understanding changing capacity require-ments for various network components as the network undergoes its dramatic expansion.

---

[1] This case was written by Charles K. Davis, University of Houston-Downtown.

Network Capacity Planning Methodology

T. J. Parker hired Sue Ellen Evans, an expert in computer systems capacity planning. During their first meeting together, Evans told Parker that "Computer and network capacity planning are closely related activities and create different views of the same information system workload. The network capacity planning methodology is an adaptation of computer capacity planning procedures. These procedures are directly applicable to the process of planning data communications networking facilities."

Evans knows that the objective of capacity planning for information systems is to assure that adequate processing capacity exists for what her previous boss used to call "the delivery system;" that is, both computing and networking services. As demand for service exceeds capacity, the quality of service for users declines rapidly. As service levels decline, it is often too late to avoid serious system performance degradation. Evans knows that network redesign and modification require too much lead time to be managed reactively. The capacity planning process must include procedures for anticipating changes in demand for networking services.

Forecasting is most reliably accomplished by the use of statistical models in a complex networking environment. Such models employ historical usage statistics for each line in the network and project trends to help identify bottlenecks in the configuration. The forecasts are then used to help design successive generations of network configurations.

The following steps recommended in Evans' final consulting report summarize the methodology developed and subsequently implemented at Southern Utility:

1.   **Document the Network.** At Southern Utility, several different inventory files of networking equipment had evolved in different departments that dealt with networking. Operations, planning, and maintenance personnel each had their own inventory lists with different items in different states of maintenance. The thrust of the documentation effort is to standardize and consolidate the inventory data into one file that can be kept current and used to report consistently across the organization. This file is the basis of inventory reporting and network topology schematics.

2.   **Review Workload Data for Systematic Fluctuations.** The utility provides electricity to customers in the Southern United States where the demand for electricity for air conditioning increases dramatically in the summer

months. This increase precipitates a dramatic increase demand for network services as the computerized billing and online customer service activities increases correspondingly.

3.   **Select Intervals for Data Collection.**   There was little historical data available at Southern Utility. Procedures were instituted to collect the data during peak periods when seasonal influences are low and this is mathematically extrapolated to gain an indication of seasonal peaks. Analysis of the data is needed for the annual information systems planning cycle before the anticipated beginning of the next seasonal increase.   The software monitor that collects the data increases the computer processing overhead significantly and degrades system performance to unacceptable levels if used to collect data during seasonal peak periods.

4.   **Identify Key Line Parameters.**   At Southern Utility, several tools were used to measure or infer response time. It was key to arrive at one set of measures that could be verified as reasonable and use them consistently in the capacity planning process over time.   It was determined that Southern Utility should acquire a network hardware monitor to improve daily network operations and to collect capacity planning data directly from the network. The hardware monitor was implemented and the data that it produced was used for network utilization reporting and forecasting on a line-by-line, subnetwork, and network-wide basis.

5.   **Review Network Protocols.**   Southern Utility decided to integrate asynchronous network protocols for office technology with the existing centralized synchronous data communications network.   Pilot studies in local area networks, integrated digital data and telephone services with gateway interfaces, were conducted to assess the addition of these facilities to the data communications network.

6.   **Establish Usage Data Base and Reporting.**   To support the network capacity planning efforts, two sets of similarly formatted network reports were developed.   One summarized short-term activity for use by network operators and

the other summarized the longer term activity for use by network planners. Both sets of reports are drawn from the same data base, employ similar formats, are demonstrably consistent, and can be periodically verified for completeness and accuracy.

7. **Profile Network Traffic.** Southern Utility had not addressed the profiling of network usage because of the difficulty of modifying existing naming conventions. Information systems executives recognize a need for profile reporting in network management and indicate a desire to pursue restructuring of the naming conventions to facilitate such reporting in the future. In the meantime, profiles of Southern Utility's workload are extrapolated from existing data and provide a basis for subsequent statistical modelling of network usage.

8. **Develop Network Simulation Models.** At Southern Utility, the initial network model included 76 high speed multipoint data communications lines. The modelling software was initialized with this network configuration and utilization statistics based upon the historical network usage data. This provides a facility for analyzing the overall performance of the network under a variety of assumptions and for highlighting potential problem areas as a prelude to network design activities.

9. **Establish Baselines and Trendlines.** The models used at Southern Utility are mostly within 15% of the actuals experienced for the test cases analyzed. This is deemed acceptable by management.

10. **Develop Planning Scenarios.** Southern Utility has utilized these forecasting techniques effectively in its annual strategic, tactical, and operational planning cycles. The company can estimate network response time averages and utilization figures by line for each of a series of changes that are under consideration. A list of either existing or potential problem areas resulting from shifts in utilization or planned modifications, such as network expansion, are now available.

11. **Evaluate Capacity, Workload, and Cost Projections.** The model at Southern Utility is used to estimate the costs for leased data communications lines between existing or planned network nodes. Total costs for alternatives are projected and various financial analyses are performed. Improvements in network analysis and design due to network capacity planning were credited with $150,000 in savings during the first year. Additionally, management believes that substantial, less tangible, benefits result from the capacity planning effort. These relate to the availability and timeliness of network management information fostered by the capacity planning approach.

12. **Present Evaluations and Recommendations for Decision-Making.** The completed analyses and recommendations were presented to information systems management for review and approval.

The consultant, Evans, has moved on to other projects in other companies after completing a successful engagement with Southern Utility. As the new Manager of Data Communications at Southern Utility, Ted Thompson is expected to keep the network development effort moving forward.

EXERCISE

1. How did the availability of personal computing based workstations impact networking at Southern Utility? What about the future?

2. How should Ted Thompson proceed? What skills does he need among his staff and how should they be organized? What should the short, medium, and long-range objectives be?

3. Which functional department at Southern Utility (e.g. Systems Planning, Administration, Network Operations, etc.) should be responsible for network planning? Why?

4. What are the unique aspects of the electric utility industry that may impact this case?

5. What additional steps are needed to adequately plan for future networking needs at Southern Utility?

CASE 18
STRUCTURING THE INFORMATION TECHNOLOGY UNIT[1]

United States Insurers (USI) was founded in 1955 by the current CEO's father and late uncle. The $40,000 in "seed money" with which the company was founded is now generating annual revenues of $603 million and USI has $6 billion in assets. Return on equity has averaged 18.9%. USI stock is publicly traded on both the New York and Tokyo Stock Exchange.

The company initially offered one product-supplemental cancer expense insurance. Currently, USI offers eight insurance products (1989 Annual Report):

(1) **Cancer Protection** - the company's first product, "designed to fill the gap between primary health insurance reimbursements and the actual costs of cancer"

(2) **Intensive Care** - covers intensive care unit expenses

(3) **Accident** - cash benefits for each day hospitalized as well as lump-sum payment (based on injury) and a death benefit

(4) **Medicare Supplement** - medical costs not covered by Medicare

(5) **Long-term Care** - for senior adults, benefits during rehabilitation at a care facility, either intermediate or custodial care

---

[1] This case was written by Charlotte S. Stephens, Columbus College, Columbus, Georgia. Published with the permission of the North American Case Research Association.

(6)   **Life Plus** - a "guaranteed-issue, cash value" policy but with benefits limited during the first two years of the policy for holders between the ages of 50 to 79 years

(7)   **Advanced Life** - term-life insurance with a "living benefit"

(8)   **LifeCare** - term-life insurance which is sold on a payroll deduction basis.

The company also has products outside the insurance industry. Its broadcast group recently sold a television station in Iowa and purchased the leading local station. Six of the seven stations owned were number one in their areas. The printing and business communications company has experienced some difficulties, but is working to capture the market in recruiting materials for U.S. colleges and universities.

Despite a broadening product base, the influence of the founders and the founding mission remains strong. The company continues to participate in niche markets, rather than in primary health care coverage or automobile insurance coverage. The company is seeking specialty products, i.e., supplementary coverage, local television stations, printing for colleges and universities, because competition is less intense with these specialty products. Furthermore, USI strives to differentiate its product by the quality of service provided to claimants and sales agents. A three day turn-around is the goal for servicing every claim.

A conservative company, this insurer has not invested in junk bonds but invests in highly liquid assets with predictable cash flows. Of the $4.6 billion in invested assets, 90-95% are highly liquid. Most insurance companies, according to the company's 1989 annual report, have 30% of their assets in junk bonds. According to the executive responsible for investments, "consistent, predictable, above-average growth is the number one goal" of his company.

Despite this conservative investment approach, marketing and distribution methods remain innovative. In fact, Forbes magazine recently named this insurer the "most innovative insurance company" of the year. Officers of USI recently testified in the U.S. Congress about their experience in penetrating the Japanese market. The differentiation of insurance products, as well as "cluster selling," were reasons for this award.

USI is a selling organization which pioneered "cluster selling" in the U.S. and Japan. While direct sales or door-to-door sales still account for about 44% of policies in the U.S., "cluster selling" or selling to employees of an organization through payroll deductions has proved more efficient and effective. In Japan, companies may legally act as the agent, selling the insurance, making payroll deductions, and earning a commission. Thus, cluster selling in Japan is known as a corporate agency system.

This marketing technique along with personal relationships cultivated by the company founder was responsible for USI's being one of the few American companies to penetrate the Japanese market.

USI Japan operates as a separate company, with its own Japanese managers and sales agents. However, great care is taken to include the Japanese culture and company in all USI publications. The company newspaper featured the founder and his wife participating in a Japanese tea ceremony. The company name on each annual report is in English and Japanese. Pursuing the Japanese market resulted from a visit to Japan, during which the founder observed that the Japanese were extremely health conscious. He began to establish personal relationships in Japan, and to become acquainted with Japanese law regarding insurance. As a result, USI Japan was established in 1974.

Cluster selling differs from group insurance in that sales are made and policies are issued to the individuals, not the company, insured. Instead of making a sales call at home, the sales call is made in the workplace. Sales exposure is maximized by being able to make group presentations. Cluster selling also leverages the high quality of USI's claimant service, increasing the persistency or continued enrollment of policy holders. With a tangible good such as a car, the car's continued performance allows the buyer to evaluate the investment continuously, notes the 1989 annual report.

With an intangible product, such as USI's specialty health insurance products, the buyer is dealing with intangibles such as "security, stability, and peace of mind." Thus, the "prompt, courteous, caring service" provided to one claimant acts as an ongoing assurance to others in the same workplace that the purchase is a good one. "Prompt, courteous, caring service" is the company's motto. This motto is prominently displayed at elevators and throughout company offices. The service mindset must permeate all those with whom the policyholder and agent interact:

> Customer evaluation of an intangible product like insurance is different. The only time a person evaluates the decision to purchase is when the policy is needed, but that need may not arise for 5 or 10 years or even longer. Therefore, it is important to reinforce the customer's purchasing decision every time he or she comes in contact with the Company. USI does this by striving to provide the absolute best customer service. We believe this begins by motivating all employees in the Home Office to understand and commit themselves to service. (1988 Annual Report)

A family feeling has been cultivated among employees, agents, and policy holders. The current CIO has worked for the company since his teens and majored in Risk and Insurance Management at a state university. His father, one of the principal founders of the company, now serves as Vice Chairman of the Board. The First Senior Vice

President has also worked for the company since his teens, also graduating from the same state university as the CEO, and his career path has also been in sales. Eight of the other twelve senior vice presidents have been with the company ten years or longer. Among the team of 17 executive management and senior vice presidents, 12, or 71%, have been with the company for ten years or longer.

The top management group is a tight knit group with long standing personal as well as professional relationships in this medium sized Southeastern city. This city was a major industrial city before the Civil War and most companies are still locally owned and managed. Those who are not natives of the area are the exception rather than the rule. The city has a substantial historic district and businesses have contributed to extensive downtown restoration.

USI is community oriented, even though its founder arrived in the city as an outsider and had to work hard to become an accepted member of the business establishment. A company newspaper and magazine encourages all employees to participate in company sponsored activities, many of which are community oriented, and keeps employees informed of the professional and personal achievements of their co-workers. The company founder and his wife are sometimes referred to as "Mr. Joe" and "Miss Ellen" in these publications.

A New Strategy

Since the early 1980's, the comfort of this family company has been disrupted by a changing environment. Health care costs have risen dramatically, consuming 10% of the U.S. Gross National Product (1989 Financial Analysts' Briefing). Providing coverage at affordable costs has become more difficult for both traditional and niche market insurers. As the population ages and health care costs increase, Medicare is being supplemented with "Medigap" products. Another critical demographic shift during the past decade has been in income distribution. According to the company's 1989 Financial Analysts' Briefing,

> Ten years ago our society was predominantly middle class, and insurance products were geared to that large market. Today, the picture is radically different. Income distribution in the U.S. shifted to the lower and higher income groups, resulting in a drastically reduced middle class. Our old cancer plan [pre-1984] was directed primarily to the middle class; the new family of cancer plans addresses the entire marketplace.

Reducing costs to provide coverage has been necessary. Consequently, downsizing and restructuring have resulted. In the 1987 annual report, the company lists 3,247 employees; in 1989, 3,005. However, sales associates supported increased from 3,800 to 4,803 in the United States. In 1983, a business strategy was formulated to respond to growing competitiveness in the insurance industry and to demographic shifts, i.e., decreasing numbers of people in the middle class as well as increasing population age. This strategy, while broadening the product base, was implemented with the company's commitment to remain the "dominant force in all the markets we serve." At the heart of the new strategy was Computer Services, now know as the Information Systems Division (ISD).

According to the current CEO, who played a major role in this new strategy, the move from a one product company to a "broader-based supplemental health insurance provider" was planned in three phases. In the first phase, existing policies were reviewed from the perspective of policy holders, sales associates, and company profitability. As a result of this review, new cancer policies were "age banded" with different rates for different age groups. The average age of policy holders had increased, causing the risk of claims to increase. Instead of increasing all premiums, age banding was implemented. The company lost many sales associates with this change. Being a sales associate is often a family affair. The company newsletters often note that a son or daughter has also joined the company as a sales associate.

In the second phase of this new strategy, an infrastructure to support product growth was implemented with new administrative and computer systems. This infrastructure has culminated in a state-of-the-art, new Data Center which "now provides computer services so good that the Company's business can be planned without regard to computing limitations," says the current Senior Vice President of ISD in a recent company newsletter. Major new systems were installed to enhance the speed and quality of customer service.

Automation provided for flexibility in the administration of products offered, with parameter changes for administrative systems essentially creating new products. Each parameter table could represent a new insurance product, from an administrative point of view. This second phase, begun in 1985 and 1986, coincides with the time the present Senior Vice President of ISD and previous Senior Vice President of ISD joined the company. Both had experience with the same insurance company prior to joining USI. One indicator of the importance of information systems planning is that the previous Senior Vice President of ISD served as chairman of the company's operating committee, a committee with major responsibility for the company's strategy.

Information systems are also an integral part of the Japan branch's operation. Although ISD services the U.S. subsidiary only, financial data is transmitted from Japan to ISD for use in corporate reports. USI Japan manages their own information systems group, but consults with the ISD as needed. The current Senior VP of US/Japan operations for insurance subsidiaries and a Senior VP of the holding company began his career as Manager of Data Processing in Japan. He then moved to the home office in the United States as the Senior VP of Computer Services.

With the new administrative and information systems infrastructure in place, the company began to broaden its product base and launched Phase III. A new logo was adopted for the insurance company, the holding company's principal subsidiary, in an effort to improve name recognition. In addition to this new product base, the ISD is now planning for the support of a reorganization of administrative functions by sales regions and for further automation of the policy assembly process.

The Senior Vice President of ISD had recently attended a five hour meeting which had been called by the CEO. Attended by the CEO, First Senior Vice President, and four other Senior Vice Presidents including the Senior Vice President of ISD, this session was intended to be an open ended "think" session. Basic questions were asked: where are we? Where are we going for the '90's? The CEO discussed three facets of operating success in the 1990's: quality, flexibility, and speed. Twenty steps to assure success were listed. The group determined that service was a major success factor which the company could control and decided that the company should provide a level of service "measurably but not extraordinarily better than the competition."

The Senior Vice President of ISD, the Senior Vice President of Administration, and two Vice Presidents who reported to the Senior VP of Administration had recently visited the vendor of an image processing system. This system was under review in the context of strategic planning. Not only would it cut labor costs in policy assembly, but also decrease the time to put a policy in the hands of a new customer. According to marketing, this turnaround would lower the number of customers who change their minds and decide not to enroll. The flexibility of the relational databases also provided the opportunity to provide new products easily and even to make computing services one of these products. The quality of customer service would also be improved, allowing customer service personnel to quickly retrieve policies on the screen whose images reflect those of the paper copy used by the customer. This system should also lower the errors associated with policy issuance and maintenance. Thus, the project embodied the three facets for success in the 1990's identified by the CEO: speed, flexibility, and quality.

Information Systems Division (ISD)

ISD is at the core of the company's effort to provide profitable insurance for specialty products across all income levels, not just middle class clients, and to provide superior service. Nevertheless, information systems remains a technical area within the company, not a career path to top management. Although senior managers support automation of insurance activities by computer based support, only two (Senior VP of ISD and Senior VP US/Japan) of the 13 senior managers have an information systems background. However, the Senior VP of Administration is an avid personal computer user both at home and work, as are many members of the Finance Department where local area networks were implemented in the mid-1980's. ISD support is for mainframe usage, for the most part. The Senior Vice President of ISD uses a personal computer as a terminal for electronic mail. The ISD remains a "mainframe shop" requiring specialization and thus some isolation.

A recent restructuring of the ISD has reduced the number of vice presidents in the division, but further isolated the programming staff from user contact. A Business Systems Analysis group provides the conceptual analysis and design for new systems. An Application Development group provides the physical design for the Programming Support group. The programming staff can be scheduled with greater flexibility and can be assigned to priority systems for the organization rather than continuing to work on projects from the functional areas to which a project group might be assigned.

This organization was recommended by consultants as a better utilization of information resources. Some users have begun to complain about having to deal with so many different people from different work groups, however. Furthermore, communications problems between the business systems analysts, applications systems analysts and programmers have surfaced. In practice, the criterion for assigning scarce resources remains problematic. Which business analysts, applications analysts, and programmers get which jobs? What is the sequence of jobs, once these jobs are assigned? Who decides that one client's job is more important than another client's job? To what extent does knowledge of the function and people in that function affect analysts' and programmers' ability to do a quality job? USI has cultivated a "family feeling," with many long term, close, personal relationships. Therefore, informal channels of communications are important. The isolation from functional units seemed to cut off analysts and programmers from these informal channels.

Furthermore, job satisfaction issues have arisen among the programming staff. While some programmers prefer the new organization in which they have minimal contact with users, others, especially the more recent graduates, report that they are less satisfied. They prefer the "whole product" approach, according to the Senior Vice President of ISD. These programmers believe that the lead time for producing would be much reduced if they were part of conceptual and physical design as well as the production, implementation, and maintenance of the system. The quality of the system service provided or its "fitness for intended use" would increase.

The Senior Vice President of ISD had informally solicited suggestions for alternative structures. One recent management information system graduate, now working as an entry level programmer trainee, had given the Senior Vice President of ISD some readings on the power of reducing work in process (WIP) and had advocated a new layout for the production of information products. This new programmer had been required to take an operations management course and had related operations management layout models to the production of information systems.

The Senior Vice President of ISD was studying these readings now. The reorganization of the information systems unit had been unsatisfactory to the previous Senior Vice President of ISD (1985-1988) and was one factor leading to his resignation. The present Senior Vice President of ISD was seeking a better solution to structuring the information technology unit, so that it could better serve the organization's new strategy. Now, the marketing effort is dependent upon computing capacity and flexibility.

At a recent ISD meeting, the Senior Vice President of ISD had challenged the employees to work toward goals that were possible only through the application of information technology. He emphasized that the ISD must play a pivotal role:

> In some insurance companies, the 4 A's-- actuarial, accounting, administrative, agency-- plan and then ask, who will tell the computer guy? In these companies, the computer guys inhibit the use of computers, not enhance it. To play a pivotal role, the computer group must be sensitive to its customers.

He reviewed the customer service survey and the persistent problem of project date deadlines not being met. He reminded them that they were actively seeking additional programmers, consultants, and independent contractors. However, he emphasized, the real answer is a long term objective:

> Returning the demand to the requester through departmental computers for the 4 A's running systems so constructed that system users can perform queries and maintain the systems by editing parameters for procedural changes. But how successful are we going to be going to the customer and saying we have a long term solution? Not very successful. I suspect that I've lost touch. I suspect that this is a perception our customers have of all of us.

EXERCISE

1.   Describe USI's culture. What are the criterion for USI's successful operation in this culture?

2.   How well does the present structure of the Information Systems Division (ISD) facilitate successful operation within this culture?

3.   Human resources in information systems are scarce. Demand exceeds supply. Therefore, job satisfaction is a key consideration in work design. Studies have shown that workers who have control of the "whole product" produce that product at higher quality levels and with greater job satisfaction. Which layout(s) would contribute to increased job satisfaction? Why?

4.   Describe the reasons for USI's change in strategy and the resulting new role for ISD.

5.   Recommend a structure or "layout" for the Information Systems Division at USI.

CASE 19
SUN MICROSYSTEMS[1]

In 1982, four individuals, who were twenty-seven years old, combined forces to found Sun Microsystems, with the objective of producing and marketing computer workstations to scientists and engineers. Two of the four were Stanford MBA graduates, Michigan born Scott McNealy, and Vinod Khosla, a native of India. They were joined by Andreas Bechtolsheim, a Stanford engineering graduate who had constructed a computer workstation with spare parts in order to perform numerical analysis, and UNIX software expert, William Joy, from the Berkeley campus. Sun's founders believed there was demand for a desktop computer workstation costing between $10,000 and $20,000 in a market niche ignored by microcomputer makers IBM, Data General, DEC, and Hewlett-Packard.

Sun Microsystems is the leader in the fast growing workstation industry expecting sales revenue growth of 30% annually during the next five years compared to 5 to 10% for the personal computer industry. Workstations can be used in stand-alone fashion or as part of networked configurations. The product lines range from low priced diskless units to higher powered graphics oriented stations at the top of the line.

In contrast to personal computers, workstations are characterized by 32 bit instead of 16 bit microprocessors, a strong tendency to use the UNIX operating system instead of MS/DOS, more sophisticated software and graphics capabilities, larger storage capacities, faster processing speeds, and the ability to function effectively in a

[1]   This case was written by William C. House, University of Arkansas and Walter E. Greene, The University of Texas-Pan American. Published with the permission of the North American Case Research Association.

networking environment. The principal users of workstations have been engineers and scientists. However, price reductions and technological improvements have broadened the appeal of workstations so that they are finding use in financial trading, desktop publishing, animation, mapping, and medical imaging applications.

Sun, the fastest growing company in the industry, has revenues that are increasing at a five year compounded rate of 85% and income increasing at 67% rate from 1985 to 1990. For fiscal year 1991, Sun's revenues were $3.2 billion and net income was $190 million. The company's rapid growth rate has severely drained its cash resources.

Chairman and CEO of Sun Microsystems

Scott McNealy, the chairman of Sun, is a native of Detroit and grew up on the fringes of the U.S. automobile industry. Originally rejected by both Harvard and Stanford Business Schools, he graduated from Harvard with a major in economics. Between his Harvard and Stanford academic careers, he worked as a foreman at Rockwell's International truck plant. After two months of hectic workplace activity, he was hospitalized with hepatitis. He entered Stanford University in 1978 on his third try.

In 1981, at the age of 26, McNealy became manufacturing director at Onyx Systems, a small minicomputer maker. The company was faced with serious quality problems. In two months, the operation showed drastic improvement as McNealy probed work rules and production bottlenecks, encouraging workers to identify problems and overcome obstacles on the way toward improving workplace efficiency.

In 1982, two former Stanford classmates, Andy Bechtolsheim and Vinod Khosla, asked him to join them as Director of Operations in a new company to be called Sun Microsystems. Two years later, McNealy was chosen by the Board of Directors to be CEO over Paul Ely, now executive vice-president of Unisys. During the first month after he became CEO, one of the three co-founders resigned, and the company lost $500,000 on two million in sales. Two-thirds of its computers didn't work.

McNealy is a workaholic, working from daylight to dark, seven days a week, rarely finding time for recreational activities. The frantic pace at Sun engendered by McNealy is sometimes referred to as Sunburn. There is a tendency for Sun executives to take on too many projects at once, thereby creating tremendous internal pressure and organizational chaos.

McNealy's philosophy can be capsulized in these company sayings:

1.   **On Decision-making**--Consensus if possible, but participation for sure.

2.   **On Management Cooperation**--Agree and commit, disagree and commit, or just get out of the way.

3.   **On Market Response**--The right answer is the best answer. The wrong answer is second best. No answer is the worst.

4.   **On Individual Initiative**--To ask permission is to seek denial.

He has stated that the company is trying to achieve four goals--significant increases in revenues and book value, improved product acceptance, and higher profit margins.

Chief Computer Designer

Andreas Bechtolsheim, chief computer designer, was one of Sun's confounders. At the age of 35, he has the title of Vice-President of technology. A native of West Germany, Bechtolsheim designed his first computer in 1980 while still a graduate student at Stanford University. It was a workstation designed for scientists and engineers. However, he was unable to sell the idea to any computer company then in existence. Shortly thereafter, he joined Joy, Khosla, and McNealy in founding Sun Microsystems and the company's first product was based on his machine.

Initially, Bechtolsheim persuaded Sun to use off-the-shelf products to develop its workstations instead of following the usual industry practice of utilizing proprietary components. This meant that company products would be easy for competitors to copy, but it allowed quick entry into the market place. As nonproprietary open systems came to be more widely accepted, competitors such as Apollo, DEC, and IBM encountered problems in keeping pace with product lines that lacked the flexibility and performance of Sun's products. When Steve Jobs formed Next, Inc. and announced the development of a desktop workstation, Bechtolsheim urged Sun officials to build a truly desktop computer. There was considerable resistance to the project and he almost left the company at that point.

Almost at once, he began working on the new computer on his own. He spent $200,000 of his own funds on the project without official company backing. He also formed a small company called Unisun to provide the vehicle for marketing his new computer and persuaded Khosla, a member of Sun's Board of Directors to become President of Unisun. Khosla offered Sun the right to invest in or purchase the smaller company outright. Sun seriously considered both possibilities, but McNealy was fearful that the new venture might be considered a competitor of Sun.

In view of the possible negatives of a smaller company selling an identical clone of Sun, the larger company finally agreed to build the new computer and call it Sparcstation 1. Initially, restrictions were placed on the project and only engineers who said that they would resign otherwise were allowed to join the project. Because the company had a culture based on building bigger boxes, the Sparcstation was widely criticized within the company as being too small. However, Bechtolsheim stubbornly refused to change the specifications and eventually prevailed.

Field Operations Director

Carol Bartz, National Sales Director and the number two executive at Sun Microsystems, has about half of the company's 12,000 employees reporting to her. Although many outsiders feel that she will soon be named chief operating officer, she abruptly dismisses the idea, observing that she doesn't believe the company needs a COO. At 42, the hard driving, aggressive sales director is reaching new heights in her career.

Bartz attended the University of Wisconsin, receiving a Bachelor of Computer Science degree in 1971. After that, she spent seven years with Digital Equipment Corporation. Since joining Sun in 1983, she has become intimately involved in marketing operations, including supervising field support activities and a subdivision that sells to federal government agencies. Bartz is a very effective problem solver, turning around a sluggish service organization and exploiting the potential in the government market.

Teams and Consensus Management at Sun

McNealy, Sun chairman, attended Cranbrook, a North Detroit prep school. While there, he excelled in a variety of activities including music, tennis, golf, and ice hockey. McNealy developed a strong self-image and competitive spirit as a result of participating in sports activities and competing with two brothers and a sister. Through the years he has approached all activities as if they were team sports.

McNealy's father, William McNealy, was the vice-chairman of American Motors. Scott followed his dad on the golf course, listened to automobile industry discussions, and found himself poring over internal company memos along with his father who was heavily involved in AMC's battle to stay alive. William McNealy ruled his household with a iron hand. McNealy's brother William, who is an architect in St. Louis, says that Scott's strong commitment to consensus management may be a reaction to the type of environment in which they were raised.

McNealy's efforts to build consensus among executives before a decision is made have become famous throughout the company. As he has stated, "Give me a draw and I'll make the decision, but I won't issue an edict if a large majority is in favor of an alternative proposal." A frequently quoted example occurred in 1988 when he stubbornly resisted changing prices at a time when rapidly increasing memory costs were reducing profit margins. With a consensus arrayed against him, he finally agreed to some product price increases which were enacted without reducing sales. In fact, he has a hard time saying no to any project pushed by one or more company groups. He demands complete loyalty within his concept of teamwork and becomes very angry if he believes that individuals or teams have let him down.

Product Line Focus

The Sparcstation 1 was introduced in April 1989 at a stripped down price of $9000. A lower priced version was introduced in May of 1990, costing $5000. The machine processes data, about twice as fast as personal computers. Sun expects the lower price to facilitate sales to companies that base computer purchases on quantity discounts. But the low end Sparcstation does not have disk drives, color monitors, or add-in slots. Therefore, it must be networked and cannot be used stand-alone.

An improved version of Sparcstation 1 was introduced in the summer of 1990 with an improved graphical interface, a color monitor, and sales price of $10,000. Sun has asserted that a personal computer with the same characteristics as the IPC would cost $15,000 to $20,000 and would have only about one third the processing power of this workstation model. The Sparcstation is now Sun's top seller among all its product lines and Sparcstation produces 80 to 90 percent of total company revenues.

Table 1 shows prices and specmarks (a measure of processing power and speed) for two Sun models as well as for the latest Hewlett Packard and IBM workstation models. From this table, relative performance of the Sun computers in terms of computing power per dollar can be compared with its major competitors.

Company Strategy

Early on, Sun executives believed that they only had a short time to focus on growing demand for computer workstations from scientists and engineers before large companies such as IBM, DEC, and Hewlett Packard would aggressively move into that market niche. Therefore, company strategy was designed to emphasize gaining market share, concentrating on all-out sales growth, no matter what the cost. At one point, the organization was adding more than 300 employees and a new sales office each

TABLE 1
A COMPARISON OF WORKSTATION PERFORMANCE MEASURES

Workstation	Price	Specmarks	Price per Specmark
Hewlett Packard 9000	11,990	55.5	216.00
Sun Sparcstation ELC	4,995	20.1	248.50
IBM RS/6000	13,992	32.8	426.50
Sun Sparcstation IPX	13,495	24.2	557.60

Source: J. A. Savage, "Price Takes a Backseat with Users," Computerworld, September 2, 1991, p. 4.

month. Company engineers developed a steady stream of innovative but sometimes impractical prototypes. Products were sold largely by word of mouth with virtually no formal sales promotion programs.

As part of the market share focus, in the mid-80's the company began creating autonomous divisions to develop and market its products. This policy allowed rapid movement into such market areas as sales to government agencies, universities, and financial institutions. A special team was created in 1986 to successfully counter the threat posed by Apollo. Sun can win market share battles in such cases, noted F. H. Moss, formerly Vice-President for software development at Apollo, because it has no strong preconceptions about what can or cannot be done. The autonomous groups did create unnecessary duplication and contributed to development costs that were almost twice the industry average. When attempts were made to consolidate functions, fierce turf battles resulted and top executives were forced to step in and referee the conflicts.

The market share/sales growth emphasis created many unexpected problems. Needed investments in customer service and data processing activities had to be postponed. The existence of independent, autonomous divisions caused numerous difficulties for both sales and manufacturing activities. At one point, the company had more than 10,000 computer and options combinations to keep track of. Three different product lines based on three different microprocessors--Sparc, Motorola 68000, and Intel 386 required excessive investment and extensive coordination to ensure that they all worked on the same network. Overlaps and duplications in marketing and finance made forecasting all but impossible. At its current size the company can no longer scramble madly to meet shipping deadlines at the last minute.

By the summer of 1989, the company was experiencing production bottlenecks as discounted sales of older products mushroomed. Demand for newer products also increased faster than expected. Large backlogs of sales orders were not being entered in the inventory control system, preventing the company from knowing how many or what kinds of products it needed to produce.

In the last quarter of 1989, Sun experienced a $20 million loss due to misjudging consumer demand for its new Sparcstation and incurring parts shortages. A new management information system produced inaccurate parts forecasts which contributed to order problems and lower earnings. However, it posted a $5 million profit in the first quarter of 1990. Sun produced revenues of $2.5 billion in fiscal 1990 and is expected to achieve revenues of $3.3 billion in 1991.

Sun is now changing its approach to place more emphasis on profitability and less on growth, on expanding customer service and hiring fewer employees. Sun President McNealy has recently tied executive pay to before tax return on investment. In the 1989 annual report he stated that he desired performance to be judged on the basis of significant increase in revenues, acceptance of new products, improvements in profit margins, and increases in book value.

McNealy was one of the early pioneers pushing open systems which would allow computers of many different manufacturers to be linked together in networks. In fact, Sun has actually encouraged competition with itself through its focus on open systems development and invited the industry to build Sparc based clones in order to expand the position of the workstation industry. As the percentage of total Sparc based computers sold by Sun has begun to decline, Sun appears to be changing its position on clones. Recently, it told its own dealers they would incur Sun's displeasure if they sold Sun clones along with the Sun workstations. Many of these dealers are angry at what they perceive to be Sun's arrogance.

Sun has consistently maintained a narrow product line focus. It has gradually phased out all microprocessors except Sparc and has concentrated on low end workstations with the greatest market share growth possibilities. It has avoided entering markets for higher priced lines and the personal computer segment with emphasis on low price and compactness. However, recently Sun announced plans to move into high end workstation markets where processing speed and power requirements necessitate linking a series of microprocessors and using sophisticated software. Sun may encounter problems in this market similar to those it experienced in product upgrades of its lower level models, since it does not have a good record in managing product introductions.

As workstations become more powerful and less expensive, workstation manufacturers face a serious challenge in maintaining profit margins. Current models now combine high functionality with high volume, in contrast to an earlier focus on producing highly functional units in small quantities. Extensive use of applications specific integrated circuits with fewer components reduces system size, increases reliability, and lowers product costs. Sun and other companies increasingly follow the practice of involving manufacturing representatives in the design process as early as possible in order to minimize manufacturing product quality and improve product testing before systems are shipped. In the past years, Sun's strategies have included focusing on lower prices, well-developed marketing programs and third party software development. From 1,500 to 2,000 applications are available for the Sun Sparcstation compared to approximately 1,000 for Hewlett Packard and DEC. The company is licensing its Sparc chip to third party clone companies with the desire of expanding the installed RISC computer base. The overall company goal is to deliver a complete processing solution, including graphics, input /output, software, and networking.

Distribution Channels and Customer Service

Workstation makers have traditionally sold their units using manufacturers sales forces and specialized hardware resellers, who repackage specialized software with other company's workstations. Sun has about 300 VARS (value added resellers) compared to more than 500 for Hewlett Packard with Digital and IBM falling somewhere in between. Some authorities think the majority of VARS are not capable of selling workstations. Sun is now considering the possibility of selling some of its models through retailers such as Microage in a manner similar to personal computer sales now made by IBM, COMPAQ, and Apple. Such a move would reduce selling and inventory costs but is meeting initial resistance from dealers unaccustomed to handling complex workstation models.

Sun still sells a large number of workstations through its 1,000 person salesforce. In July 1990, Sun selected 200 dealers from three retail chains and gave them training in selling workstations. The company expects to sell 30 million dollars of workstations through retail dealers in Fiscal 1990, but a full-fledged dealer network may require several years to develop. Because of the higher average selling prices and of greater product differentiation and uniqueness of workstations compared to personal computers, many PC vendors are expressing interest in handling workstations in spite of the small volumes generated.

One area of concern has been Sun's field service organization which has not been very effective in supporting customer software. Bartz has stated that the company wants to improve on customer service without making large monetary expenditures or building a dinosaur service group. In line with this, Sun announced plans to start using company-trained, third-party service personnel who can be dispatched to customer locations on demand.

Customer Categories

The workstation market for engineers and scientists is rapidly becoming saturated. About one-third of Sun's customers now come from the commercial side, up from only 10% several years ago. The company is now concentrating more of its efforts on airlines, banks, insurance and finance companies, trying to persuade users to utilize Sun workstations to solve new problems. Sun Vice-President Eric Schmidt says that Sun tends to get early adopters of new technology. Often, by starting with a pilot program that proves successful, workstations can be expanded to other areas in a customer's operations. Eastman Kodak began using Sun workstations in engineering design and soon expanded their use of marketing databases and mailroom operations.

Sun machines are being used by Wall Street firms, Merrill Lynch, Shearson/Lehman/-Hutton and Bear/Sterns, on the trading floor. Northwest Airlines uses 500 workstations in Minneapolis to monitor ticket usage, checking the correctness of air fare changes and the impact of flight delays or cancellations on revenues and profits. To increase customer satisfaction, Sun has had to change product designs, to make its machines easier to install, and improve readability of product manuals. As Sun has discovered, commercial customers need more help than engineers.

Dataquest says that by 1994, 29.1% of workstation sales will be made to commercial users as opposed to Scientific/Engineering users in a market expected to reach $22 billion. Workstation manufacturers are moving into the personal computer area by offering UNIX versions that will run on both workstations and on personal computers. Workstations provide much greater computing power at a lower cost than would be required to enhance a personal computer so that it possessed the equivalent capability of a typical workstation. Workstations seem to be making their biggest inroads into CPU intensive applications formerly done on mainframes (e.g., stock transactions, airline reservations).

Sun's first major TV advertising effort occurred in April 1991 and took the form of the 30 second commercial seen on CNN, ESPN, and the three major TV networks. The commercial was not directed specifically at a consumer audience, but instead was an attempt to get broad exposure for a new message beamed at the business market. Sun expected the advertisement to reach 59% of U.S. households and 42% of the target market of senior level corporate executives. The campaign also included an eight page insert in the Wall Street Journal.

Sun's advertising budget of approximately $4.6 million in 1990 was spent on computer and general interest business publications. Sun's advertising budget is only about 0.25% of sales revenue compared to 1.0 to 1.5% spent by its major competitors. Some observers have questioned the cost-effectiveness of a high priced TV advertisement by a company which sells high priced computers to a limited group of customers.

Software Developments

Availability of software still remains a major problem in expanding sales of workstations. Only about 5% to 10% of UNIX based software is designed for business and commercial applications. Sun is trying to sign up software developers to produce UNIX based versions of many common personal computer products. It now has UNIX based versions of popular PC software, including Lotus 1-2-3 and DBASE IV. It hopes the increased availability of software plus the narrowing cost gap between low end work-stations and high end personal computers will help it penetrate the personal computer market. However, it must sell users on the benefit/cost performance of workstations compared to personal computers and also needs to expand its existing base of software developers.

The type of software to run is often the determining factor in deciding between a personal computer or workstation. For productivity and business applications, PCs can be more cost efficient. For technical and graphics applications, workstations are more appropriate. Differences in costs are no longer a differentiating factor.

An entrenched personal computer MS/DOS operating systems base and lack of commercial workstation software has hampered a switch from high-end personal computers to workstations. MS/DOS based computers appear adequate for a majority of user needs, especially with the advent of the WINDOWS operating environment. PC users are more likely to change if complex applications such as multimedia, integrated database, or windowing become desirable rather than on the basis of price alone. Workstations may become less attractive if 80846 based personal computers with considerably more computing power than today's systems become more widely available.

Product/price performance is no longer as important a factor as it used to be. Software availability and usability is increasing in importance. In recognition of this, Sun has formed two software subsidiaries--one for application software and one to concentrate on improvements in the UNIX operating system. The Open Look Graphical Interface has been added to make Sun products more user friendly. The key to maintaining market position seems to be improving systems software and selling software developers and users on the benefits of workstations over other hardware options.

Sun has announced that it will release a new version of its operating system designed to run on Intel based personal computers. Some analysts say that Sun will face a stiff test in competing with Microsoft's DOS/Windows combination and that it is a defensive move, made in realization that Sun no longer can generate enough revenue from its own machines to meet its growth goals. McNealy denies that the Sun announcement is defensive, saying that high powered PC owners will move to Sun's operating systems to take advantage of advanced capabilities (e.g., running multiple programs simultaneously) which is something that has been vaguely promised by Microsoft's Windows new NT versions. McNealy has sharply criticized Windows NT version, referring to it as illusionary or not there.

Sun's Solaris operating systems will not be available until mid-1991, and will work on both Intel's X86 series and Sun's Sparc processors. The new operating system will make it easier for Sun's customers to link Sun workstations with other computers in a network and increase the number of Sun users. Sun hopes that this will encourage software houses to write new programs for Sun's OS. So far, approximately 3,500 application programs are available for Sun OS compared with more than 20,000 for IBM-compatible personal computers.

Competition in the Marketplace

Although still the market leader, Sun is facing increasing competition from much larger computer companies. Sun shipped 146,000 workstations in 1990 (39% of the market) out of a total of 376,000 and is expected to ship 200,000 in 1991. Having fully absorbed Apollo into its organization, Hewlett Packard is selling about two-thirds as many workstations as Sun, with about 20% of the market and DEC, which has completely reworked its product lines, has about 17% of the workstation market. Hewlett Packard has also introduced a new workstation model comparable in price to Sparcstation which runs about twice as fast as Sun's current model. Table 2 shows the 1989 and 1990 market shares for the major firms in the workstation market.

IBM has made a significant comeback in the workstation market with the RS/6000, after its first workstation model proved to be a slow seller. In 1990, IBM shipped more than 25,000 workstations, producing revenues of one billion dollars and a market share of 6.6%, or more than double its 1989 market share. In 1991, some analysts estimate IBM will sell between two to three billion dollars of workstations. IBM has a stated goal of overtaking Sun by 1993, achieving a 30% market share, although some experts predict it is more likely to achieve a 15% market share by that date.

With the workstation market expected to exceed $20 billion by the mid-1990's, competition is expected to be fierce. IBM'S late entry, entrenched positions of competitors in the market, lack of a low-priced entry-level model, and use of nonstandard operating and graphics environments are likely to hamper its efforts to achieve a market share much above 15%. IBM's service and sales reputation, its large reseller base, and strong position in commercial markets should give the company leverage to enter the fast growing markets for network servers and small or branch office multiuser systems. However, if IBM focuses its efforts on penetrating these markets with its RS/6000, it runs a serious risk of undercutting sales of the AS/400.

TABLE 2
COMPUTER WORKSTATION MARKET SHARES

	Percent Market Share	
Company	1989	1990
Sun Microsystems	30.4	38.8
Hewlett Packard	26.1	20.1
Digital Equipment	26.6	17.0
Intergraph	7.0	3.8
Silicon Graphics	5.1	2.6
Sony	-	3.3
Next	-	2.6
Other	3.6	7.0
Total	100.0	100.00

Cost is no longer the primary factor in decisions to acquire workstations. Workers must become more accustomed to graphic-as opposed to character-based systems before adoption by the current PC users becomes more widespread. Some companies feel that workstations have yet to demonstrate significant productivity advantages over personal computers. The biggest shortcomings of workstations are lack of application software and integration difficulties.

EXERCISE

1. In the face of increased competition and saturation of the markets, should Sun emphasize its higher priced or lower priced workstation lines? Should Sun target its lower priced workstations against high-end personal computers, promoting and selling through retailers in a manner similar to personal computer makers? Why?

2. Evaluate Sun's performance in terms of stated company objectives -- i.e., significant revenue increases, product acceptance, improved profit margins, and book value increases. How does Sun's performance compare with industry averages?

CASE 20
SYSTEMATICS INC.[1]

After experiencing dramatic growth by providing financial services to both American and foreign banks since its formation in Little Rock, Arkansas in 1968, Systematics Incorporated now faces many internally and externally generated problems and opportunities. Since it was acquired by ALLTEL Corporation in May, 1990 for $528.0 million in stock, Systematics has suddenly obtained access to a vast amount of capital that it can use to pursue additional growth avenues. For its part, ALLTEL expects its average annual five-year growth rate of 10.0% to be greatly enhanced by Systematics' 21.1% rate while simultaneously capturing various operating and technological synergies.

In the face of this pressure for profits and growth, John Steuri, President and Chief Executive Officer of Systematics, must deal with several violent changes occurring in the banking industry which some describe as a general sickness associated with America's banking institutions. In recent years profit performance has been low or negative, much of the banking public has lost confidence in the system's strength and integrity, and massive consolidations and mergers have been completed in attempts to seek either safety in size or to obtain various operating economies or portfolio diversifications. These problems have affected Systematics which is a major supplier of software and other financial services to over 800 banks in forty-five states and nearly twenty countries.

---

[1]   This case was written by Joseph Wolfe, The University of Tulsa, based on a graduate student research project conducted by Robert Knapp.

How Systematics should respond to these pressures has divided its management team. Many feel the company should stick to the banking industry which has been the source of its past successes. Other executives feel they must capitalize on ALLTEL's strengths as a telephone holding company that has diversified into cellular telephone and other communications services.

The Bank Financial Services Industry

In 1980 the ABA Banking Journal sensed the development of a new trend in bank operations management. Given an average sized bank devotes about 8.0% of its expenses to data processing (DP), various economies could be realized by a bank if this work could be "farmed out" to a more efficient data processor. Five forces seem to be driving this development:

1. **The scarcity and high price of technical talent**--Many banks find it difficult to attract and hold DP personnel and must buy off-the-shelf software or contract outside technical labor.

2. **Pressure for more sophisticated applications**--as technological capabilities increase, banks, as well as their customers, wish to realize the cost and convenience advantages these technologies can bring to an operation.

3. **Greater competition from bank saturation or industry deregulation**-- competition is fierce between the savings and loan banks versus commercial banks and credit unions. Small banks attempt to match the services provided by the larger banks which attempt to prevail by providing the best services available.

4. **Pressure for profits**--As various markets converge and growth cannot come from increased revenues, banks must find profit sources through operating efficiencies.

5. **Changes in the capabilities of those offering financial services to the banking industry**--computer service companies have grown in size and financial stability, thus becoming dependable suppliers of DP skills and applications. Many service organizations have created software and possess technical talent which can only be duplicated by an individual bank at a very high cost.

It has been estimated that by 1994 this trend will result in the doubling of the industry to one with sales of over $2.6 billions or an annual growth rate of over 17.0% per year. This growth has occurred mainly among the smaller institutions although various industry experts feel the trend may spread to the larger banks once they succumb to the natural pressures building within the industry.

A bank's data processing system helps in the delivery of many bank services:

1. **Basic operations**--This entails keeping track of teller operations, handling demand and time-deposit accounting, and processing installment and mortgage loan applications and payments.

2. **Trust services**--Manages the various investments contained in customers' trust portfolios.

3. **Financial analysis**--Poses "what if" questions to aid in the selection and balancing of investment portfolios owned by either bank customers or the bank itself.

4. **Automated customer services**--Handles the accounting and electronic operation of the bank's automated teller machines.

5. **Specialized services**--These services vary from bank to bank based on the clientele it wishes to cultivate and special needs associated with that clientele. Once this audience is identified, the operations associated with this group are automated through computer support.

Banks have historically attempted to solve their data processing needs three ways. Some have done all the work themselves, from programming to computer operations, with in-house personnel. This has been difficult to do even by the largest banks. Most banks use what is called a double approach. They employ outside services for their routine DP work while using in-house personnel to handle their unique or critical needs. A third approach has been to completely rely upon third-party consulting firms to perform all DP work. These firms range from general accounting firms to specialized DP management consulting companies.

Just as competition within the banking industry has increased, competition between those servicing the industry has also increased. More than 640 vendors supply the industry and these vendors differ regarding their product strategies. Some can satisfy all of a bank's data processing needs, while others offer a more limited variety of products or services. Those products and services are the following:

1.   **Software packages**--These are pre-programmed computer programs purchased by the bank rather than having the bank create its own programs with in-house personnel. The DP servicer's range of participation can vary from merely selling the software off-the-shelf to installing and customizing the product (with in its own preprogrammed limitations) to meet the bank's specific needs.

2.   **Remote computing services**--These are mainframe computer time-sharing operations in which banks use on-line computing through an off-site computer via office terminals in a real time mode.

3.   **Remote batch processing**--This is a slower data processing method which involves the bank entering data on-site and sending it to a central computer that will process the data overnight and redistribute the information the following day.

4.   **Turnkey purchase**--This method does not entail the direct purchase of equipment or software by the bank but instead has the vendor select the equipment, program it, get it up and running, while providing on-going maintenance once the bank itself has taken custody of the operation.

5.   **Facilities management**--This is the most comprehensive set of services a vendor can provide. In this method the vendor assumes full responsibility for hiring and training operators, installing and running the computer, programming all bank computer applications, and delivering results according to the basic contract in force between the bank and the facilities management supplier.

Figure 1 outlines the products and services offered by several firms in the information technology industry while Figure 2 outlines the characteristics of some of the industry's major competitors. Among the top ten suppliers seven sell application software, nine offer data processing services of some kind, and three offer facilities management. In 1990, the aggregate revenues for these firms were $3.7 billion. This was a 32.0% increase over the prior year although this increase was less than the 50.0% increment that occurred between 1987 to 1988.

Given the banking industry's rather bleak profit situation, a strong cost control trend has exerted itself. As observed by Frank Martire, Chairman of Citicorp Information Resources, a devilish dilemma exists with in the industry.

> What we hear-and we talk regularly to a couple of hundred bankers across the country-is cost control, and it's not different by size of bank or location-it's across the country. If banks can delay investments, they're going to do it, but intelligent banks with real foresight are not going to try to control costs so much that it harms service to the customer. They still want to position the right product or right service for a recovery, which will come in 1993 or 1994.

Accordingly, banks have begun to look more intensely at the financial service industry's offerings. Extreme concentration has been placed on maximizing short-term efficiency combined with major, long-term technological improvements. Many feel this will lead to an increase in banking's search for alliances and technology partners to aid in sharing the costs and risks of technological advancement during a period of severe cost control.

Systematics Inc.

Systematics Inc. was founded by Walter Smiley after having been a systems engineer for IBM and an eight-year data processing manager for the First National Bank of Fayetteville, Arkansas. By 1977 its sales had grown to $13.3 million after having begun as an eight person company just nine years before. In 1980 the company began to market software packages to banks other than the one it was servicing in Fayetteville and by 1981 its sales had reached $36.3 million. Shortly after that Systematics began to service international customers and Smiley began to voluntarily take on a less-dominant role within the company.

In August 1988 John Steuri took over Smiley's position as Systematics' CEO. Steuri was himself a 24-year IBM veteran beginning as a sales representative in Topeka, Kansas and ultimately headed an IBM marketing force of 9,000 people doing more than $6.0 billion worth of business a year. Systematics was an attractive opportunity for him when he left IBM at the age of 49 with an attractive early-out package.

> The qualities I admired in IBM were evident in Systematics. It was a well-run, focused, growth-oriented company with a commitment to customer service. Systematics also was still small enough that I felt I had a chance to be a part of a real entrepreneurial enterprise.

FIGURE 1
PRODUCTS AND SERVICES OFFERED BY SELECTED BANK VENDORS

Vendor	1989 Revenue (in Millions)	Products and Services
Electronic Data Systems Plano, TX	900.0	Application software, Turnkey systems, Local batch processing, Remote non-interactive processing, Interactive processing, Facilities Management, Custom programming, Consulting, Education/Training
First Financial Management Atlanta, GA	741.0	Application software, Turnkey systems, Local batch processing, Remote non-interactive processing, Interactive processing, Custom programming, Consulting, Education/Training
Systematics Little Rock, AR	224.7	Application software, Remote non-interactive processing, Interactive processing, Turnkey systems, Facilities Management, Custom programming, Consulting
Mellon Information Services Pittsburgh, PA	170.9	Applications software, Interactive processing
NCR Dayton, OH	168.1	Applications software, Interactive processing, Custom programming, Consulting, Education/Training
SunGard Data Systems Wayne, PA	125.0	Applications Software, Interactive processing
Citicorp Information Resources Stamford, CT	104.0	Turnkey systems, Interactive processing, Facilities management, Custom programming
Unisys Houston, TX	99.9	Applications software, Consulting
BISYS Houston, TX	54.2	Facilities management, Custom programming, Consulting
The Kirchman Corporation Orlando, FL	54.0	Applications software, Local batch processing, Education/Training
National Computer Systems Eden Prairy, MN	38.4	Turnkey systems
Financial Information Trust West Des Moines, IA	31.1	Interactive processing

Source: Adapted from "America's Top Fifty Banking Software Products," Banking Software Review, Autumn 1990, pp. 28-31.

FIGURE 2
COMPANY SKETCHES

ELECTRONIC DATA SYSTEMS (EDS)--This company has been providing services in general for more than 25 years to all 50 states and 27 countries. They attempt to create solutions, through their 2,000 employees, that best accomplish the individual financial institution's goals while still maintaining EDS's unique corporate personality. EDS offers an almost complete line of services including such others as systems integration and communications facilities management. Because of its size it can process more than 3.0 billion instructions per second, 24 hours a day, 365 days a year. It can transmit voice, data, and video around the world using terrestrial, satellite, microwave, and fiber optic technology.

IBM CORP.--IBM brings its image of reliability plus its dominance of the mainframe computer to the financial services industry. It is a prime contractor in many banks, but daily operations are sub-contracted to a third party vendor. IBM's marketing strategy involves tailoring each contract to the customer's individual requirements; it refuses to use the term "facilities management" as it implies an off-the-shelf approach that they reject.

SOFTWARE ALLIANCE--Software Alliance markets its UNIX-based Total Banking Solution to small to medium sized banks while it markets its Marshall & Isley Integrated Banking System to larger banks. The company's software interfaces with all IBM compatible computers. Rather than developing their own applications, Software Alliance obtains the marketing rights from successful software developers. After obtaining these rights it targets banks with up to $750.0 million in assets and a second group of those with assets ranging from $2.0 to $200.0 billion.

NEWTREND MISER2--Founded in 1977 this company's software consists of over 40 deposit, loan, customer service, financial control, management support, and EFT/ATM applications all operating on Unisys hardware. Newtrend's components are not sold individually. Customers purchase an integrated core system to which modules are added as needed. The company is well known for individually customizing its integrated system which is available through in-house use, a service bureau, or facilities management.

THE KIRCHMAN CORPORATION--Kirchman claims over 6,000 clients and it allocates approximately 20.0% of its gross revenues to research and development. The company operates solely on IBM machines designed for single or multibank environments. Their newest product is called Dimension Software which is an integrated system for small to medium-sized banks.

TABLE 1
SYSTEMATICS INC. ACTUAL AND FORECASTED REVENUES
(In Millions of Dollars)

Year	Revenues
1985	$ 95.9
1986	122.6
1987	141.6
1988	179.5
1989	206.8
1990	254.8
1991	305.5
1992	365.0
1993	440.0

Note: Revenues after 1991 are Yankee Group estimates.

Source: 10-K Reports and The Yankee Group, 1991.

TABLE 2
SYSTEMATICS INC. OPERATING INCOME
(In Millions of Dollars)

Year	Operating Income
1985	$ 15.0
1986	17.0
1987	20.0
1988	28.0
1989	32.0
1990	34.0

Source: Company stockholder reports.

Sales have continued to grow and many expect, as shown in Table 1, that its revenue prospects are very bright. Table 2 displays the income from operations obtained by Systematics. Industry experts feel the firm's strengths lie in the integrated, IBM-based COBOL software it possesses as well as in its reputation for quality service. The software addresses a wide range of applications, including deposits, loans, profitability analysis, branch automation, electronic funds transfer, and marketing. Its newest product is entitled Extended Application Architecture (EAA) and it allows banks to migrate to new technologies, such as regional databases, in an orderly manner when it becomes cost effective. Systematics has also begun to offer an Advanced Loan System which was created with the EAA. This is a comprehensive loan servicing system that allows users to introduce new loan products with little programming support. It also offers many debt management features not offered by other systems.

Systematics delivers its products three ways depending on the size of the bank being serviced. First, it provides facilities management and data processing services for 390 American and foreign bank clients. Second, it sells its applications software to financial institutions for their in-house use. Third, they sell turnkey operations consisting of mid-range systems and applications software through an IBM remarketing agreement.

Approximately 75.0% of its revenues are derived from facilities management. In December 1990 Systematics Inc. signed a 10-year service contract valued at between $350.0 and $500.0 million with the City National Bank of Beverly Hills, CA and another contract to operate First New Hampshire Banks' data processing center was announced in February 1991. As of January 1991 Systematics had over 80 on-site financial management agreements.

To some degree the banking industry's generally poor financial condition, plus the closing or consolidation of smaller banks which are an important target group for Systematics Inc., has had an effect on the company's thinking. Steuri, however, saw a silver lining in this cloud.

> Everyone knows there is a general malaise in the financial sector. Granted, that hurts our software sales, which accounted for only 10 to 12 percent of our business last year. There is another side though. If they turn their data processing over to us, we can help them. We can reduce their costs at least 10 to 15 percent and put money on their bottom line real fast.

Despite the industry's doldrums Systematics met its 12-month goal for facilities management contracts within the first nine months of the 1990 fiscal year. In fact Steuri has said "There have been occasions when our sales reps have been sent home for a week or two so we would not sign more contracts than we could service."

ALLTEL Enters the Picture

With its acquisition by another Little Rock, Arkansas company, Systematics, Inc. became part of a $1.57 billion operation with diversified interests in cellular telephone systems, natural gas service, air traffic control voice switching and control systems, signal data converters, encrypted voice communications systems, and high resolution color graphic display systems. Table 5 shows that Systematics would garner about 16.0% of ALLTEL's total sales, but would contribute more than that percentage to its operating income. Accordingly Joe Ford, ALLTEL's President and CEO called this acquisition "one of the most significant of our strategic moves". Various industry observers are more skeptical about the acquisition and its long-term benefits to either company. James Stork, a security analyst for Duff & Phelps Inc. stated:

> There are really no strategic reasons or synergies here. We do not view this as a strategic acquisition, although data processing and telecommunications may be converging, it is difficult to see how the combination of these two companies will result in much in the way of synergy over the next five years. We get the impression that ALLTEL acquired Systematics simply because it became available, and ALLTEL felt it could increase its consolidated growth potential for a reasonable price.

Both John Steuri and Joe Ford have begun to rise to the occasion. Steuri says "we foresee some potential synergies as the communications and computer industries continue to converge". Because there are about 1,300 telephone companies currently competing in the United States, he felt they could be approached by the same sales pitch used when they recruited banks and savings and loan institutions. "Let us do your data processing for you. We can do it cheaper and more efficiently than you can do it in-house."

In this quest for synergies between the two companies Systematics completed a deal in March 1991 to acquire C-TEC Corporation's cellular telephone billing and information system and ALLTEL turned its cellular data processing operation over to Systematics. ALLTEL has also begun to sell off various operations not related to telecommunications and information processing. It sold its natural gas distribution systems in Nevada and California to Southwest Gas Corporation for $16.0 million in June 1991 and it is attempting to sell off its Ocean Technology, Inc. subsidiary as well as its alternate energy investments.

Although moves are being made to make this a successful acquisition for ALLTEL, and John Steuri feels pressure is being placed on him to help his new parent corporation realize its own growth goals, he thinks numerous diverse factors need to be considered. Admittedly the banking industry is in a state of turmoil but Systematics' business strengths lie within that industry.

EXERCISE

1. What competitive forces exist in the bank financial services industry? What are the key success factors in this industry?

2. Should the company attempt to ride out the banking industry's storm while possibly incurring the wrath of ALLTEL's management for failing to move ahead with applications in the telecommunications industry?

3. Could Systematics attempt to fill other product/services niches in the banking industry despite the awesome size of its major competitors?

4. Does Systematics have any other options?

CASE 21
TUCKERS' TRACTORS[1]

"I'm Mrs. Tucker. My son, Jimmy, and I own Tuckers' Tractors."

"Come in Mrs. Tucker, and have a seat. Your son Jimmy made the appointment. Is he going to join us?"

"Jimmy is at the shop, he'll be here in just a minute." Mrs. Tucker began telling me about the business. She and Jimmy were excited about free computer-related consulting. "Our business has needed a computer for a long time. Margaret does all our bookkeeping and invoicing by hand."

Jimmy was twenty minutes late. "I'll just see if he's on his way," she said reaching across for the phone. A quick phone call reminded Jimmy of our appointment.

"My husband died about three years ago. Thank goodness I had Jimmy. I wouldn't have been able to run the business without him -- my daughter lives in Texas."

"Mrs. Tucker was just giving me some background information," I told Jimmy as he joined us. "Why don't you start by telling me why you need a computer?"

Jimmy didn't hesitate, "Margaret Case, our bookkeeper, is overcome by paperwork. We need to automate her office. Our biggest problem is accounts receivable. People

[1] This case was written by Kirk E. Stephens, Southwestern Community College; and Jo Ann C. Carland and James W. Carland, Western Carolina University. Published with the permission of the North American Case Research Association.

aren't paying on time, some don't pay at all. A computer would also help us manage and order our parts inventory."

"Margaret is very excited," added Mrs. Tucker, "and I'm sure she would have no trouble doing the books and the payroll with a computer. We might even be able to eliminate the part-time girl who helps out after school."

Background of the Company

Tuckers' Tractors is a small, privately owned company located in a rural, eastern Tennessee town. The firm sells and services farm tractors. Tuckers' is an authorized dealer of Ford, Kubota, and Massey-Ferguson product lines. It is the only dealer in farm tractors within a 100 mile radius.

Tuckers' Tractors sells primarily to small farmers in a four county area in Eastern Tennessee. The number of farmers in the area has been declining over the last two decades. The remaining farmers, all of whom own farm tractors, tend to purchase new equipment infrequently. Consequently, much of the current sales revenues come from repairs and service to existing costumers rather than from the sale of tractors.

Management

Tuckers' Tractors was founded in the 1940s by James Tucker who operated it as a sole proprietorship. During the next 25 years, the firm prospered under Tucker's aggressive sales and management styles. In the late 1960s, James, Jr. (Junior) took over management of the family business, later becoming the sole owner at his father's death. Industry sales were lower during this period, but Tuckers' Tractors had a loyal client base and had been depending upon repeat sales for some time. In fact, all of Tuckers' competition failed during this period. Junior recognized the problem and moved to maintain revenues by expanding Tuckers' service department. Tuckers' survived and tractor maintenance and repair is the majority of Tuckers' business today.

James Tucker, III (Jimmy) is a third generation manager for the firm. His father's early death has placed him at the helm of a partnership. Other partners are Jimmy's sister, his mother and his Uncle Robert, Junior's younger brother, each of whom inherited a one fourth interest in the firm at Junior's death. The sister is a silent partner and has never been involved with the business on any level, but Mrs. Tucker "helps out" occasionally. Prior to her husband's death, Mrs. Tucker's only contact with the business had been the weekly Friday ritual of coming to the office to collect Junior's check. Jimmy, currently 35 and unmarried, has worked in the family business full-time since he finished high school. He dabbled in sales, repairs and clerical work, but he never held a management position. At his father's death three years ago, Jimmy became the primary manager for the business and was suddenly thrown into a world that he had never experienced.

Financial Information

When the subject of financial performance arose, Jimmy remarked that tractor sales had been flat for the last three years. Repair sales have been declining and now they are having trouble meeting payroll.

Mrs. Tucker cut him off before he could disclose any further financial information. She said, "Since I'm only concerned with buying a computer and I know that I can afford that; you don't need to know any other details of the company."

I quickly assured her that she did not need to give me any more information than she felt inclined to give. I stressed that it would help me to assess her situation more fully and I would be able to suggest more appropriate computer alternatives, if I were more familiar with the company and its financial condition. After all, I explained, any computer system would entail some cost.

Mrs. Tucker, then, told me about Uncle Robert. Uncle Robert is Mrs. Tucker's brother-in-law and he was left a quarter of the business upon the death of her husband. Mrs. Tucker and Uncle Robert were adversaries and apparently had always been so. Robert, 55 years old, had been a salesman for 38 years, beginning work with the company as a young man shortly after Junior had been brought in by their father.

Soon after Junior's death, it became quite apparent that Uncle Robert and Mrs. Tucker could not function together within the company. Mrs. Tucker proposed that Uncle Robert sell his share of the business to the partnership. Their negotiations resulted in a price which was so high that Mrs. Tucker refused to reveal the amount. Apparently, Uncle Robert set his own price. An additional stipulation of the sale was that Robert be permitted to remain with Tuckers' as a commissioned salesman as long as he wished. Knowing that Robert would be totally removed from management and that his only salary draws would be based on commissions, Mrs. Tucker agreed.

While this information was coming out, Jimmy was silent. He had clearly not been involved in the negotiations, but he took over the story at this point. "Uncle Robert hasn't made a dime in commissions, but he is still bleeding the company dry! His monthly payment for the buy back took every penny last month!"

Mrs. Tucker deftly moved the conversation away from the subject of Uncle Robert with the admonition, "It's worth it to be rid of his meddling!" No amount of questioning at this or at any future interview could elicit any further financial information.

Operations

Tuckers' Tractors is a large facility of some 6,000 square feet, located on a level lot with paved drive and parking lot about one and one half miles from a small town of 20,000 people. The town is the largest in the county, or within the four county area. The main entrance is a showroom for farming tractors. There is a lounge area with couch, chair and access to brochures of the full line of products available from Tuckers' Tractors. Since this is the same facility built by James, Sr. in the 1940s, not much has changed. Even the furniture shows years of use.

Jimmy, seeing my reaction to the showroom and lounge remarked, "You have to remember that farmers don't expect to have to dress up to come get their tractors fixed." A full time salesman is available to handle customers, but Jimmy also sells in his absence. Uncle Robert was not in sight.

The area directly beyond the showroom contains shelves of tractor accessories and parts for the do-it-yourself mechanic. The parts desk is located to the right of the main entrance. The parts department has two windows, one facing customers in the retail area and another for the mechanics in the shop in the rear of the building. The parts manager maintains a record of all parts sold at retail or used in repairs. The shop, occupying the rear half of the building, employs three mechanics and a foreman. Used parts that have been returned or salvaged from repairs are stacked and piled against the back wall of the shop. There are two bay doors in the side of the building that open to the shop. Two tractors were under repair in the shop during our visit, one of which looked as if it might have been sold by James, Sr. when he first opened the business. Offices for Tuckers' Tractors are located upstairs over the parts department. All accounting, invoicing, and record keeping is done by a single person in the office.

Record Keeping

"Margaret Case is our central nervous system," Jimmy said as he introduced me to the bookkeeper. "Ms. Case has been with us forever; she really runs this business."

Jimmy had a customer, so I used that opportunity to speak with Mrs. Case. "How could we improve your system?" I asked.

Mrs. Case responded immediately. "The biggest problem is our accounts payable. The parts manager orders parts, but I get the invoices. There's no way to get a good check of what's come in and what's still on order. But worst of all, I have to send a letter to all our customers who have an account each month. There are more and more accounts and it takes longer and longer each month."

"You carry accounts for your customers?" I had known from Jimmy that some accounts receivable existed, but I had not expected a large number.

"Mr. Tucker knew that his customers had to have credit until their crops came in and no one would give it to them. This business was built on the idea that a good customer was worth waiting on! That means that we carry accounts for almost all of our customers' repairs. Any new tractors that we sell get financed by the Ford company, but we handle accounts for about everything else." Mrs. Case opened a drawer in a filing cabinet. It was filled, as were three other drawers with customer account files. Surprised at the volume, I explained to her that the computer Jimmy wanted could help with billing and keeping track of customer accounts.

"Jimmy's not going to get a computer, they cost too much and the business can't afford it," Mrs. Case emphasized. A bit taken aback at her insistence that no computer would be forthcoming for Tuckers' Tractors, I went in search of Mother Tucker.

EXERCISE

From a systems management consultant's viewpoint complete the following:

1. Can this company survive, with or without a computer?

2. Who is the 'real boss' in this firm? What indicates this knowledge to you?

3. What is causing the financial problem with the firm?

4. What situation gives you an indication that the consultants are going to have a difficult time with this client? What is the probable outcome of the above situation?

5. What would be some recommendations for this company if it were feasible to make suggestions about the business?

6. What suggestions would you make as the consultant about the appropriate computer system for this firm?

CASE 22
USING INFORMATION TECHNOLOGY FOR COMPETITIVE ADVANTAGE[1]

It was Friday, 7:00 p.m., and the two of them stood talking in an almost deserted parking lot. The Chief Information Officer (CIO), known to everyone from computer operators to the CEO as "Charlie," challenged the consultant: "Tell me what you believe I need to do. I don't want to retire to the same tune we heard today. An outsider should be able to provide some insights which those in the fray of the battle cannot see. Can you get back to me on Monday? As you observed today, our situation is critical. We've got to reduce the risks without sacrificing the rewards of our strategy."

Lithonia Lighting's CIO and CEO were business heroes. Friends since high school, they had attended college together. While the CIO worked for a national computer company, the CEO completed an MBA at Harvard University. They had been with Lithonia Lighting (LL) for twenty-four of its forty-four years and had helped the company move from a small, Southern lighting company to a national presence in the commercial/industrial lighting market.

Information technology had been used to create a sustained competitive advantage. More than a support function automating clerical and accounting functions, information technology had been used as a marketing weapon. LL had fought the battles to make new technology work, placed microcomputers in agent's offices, networked these microcomputers, and adapted the client-server architecture long before these techniques were touted in business periodicals.

---

[1]   This case was written by Charlotte S. Stephens, Columbus College, Columbus, Georgia. Published with the permission of the North American Case Research Association.

181

The rewards of early adaptation of this new technology had been great. The service provided by these field systems had differentiated the LL products and raised barriers to entry in the market. But the risks were great as well. If a system failed, the company could lose business, not merely suffer the annoyance of a late report.

The CIO had been told by the Senior VP of Marketing that the same systems which had provided a competitive advantage in the market place were now experiencing so many problems that the effect was backfiring. A Dothan, Alabama, agent had already switched to another supplier out of frustration with system failures. The West coast, especially Los Angeles, had also experienced failures. In fact, the Distribution Manager had encouraged distribution centers and warehouses to use facsimile machines to deliver orders and shipping verifications instead of using the order processing system in place.

A prominent Los Angeles agent, a former LL executive and a Harvard MBA, had written the CEO a long letter detailing the problems he had experienced and he had proposed solutions. The CIO agreed with the problems but thought the solutions would cause a loss of data integrity, and eventually, a disintegration of information validity.

The consultant agreed to take the job. She decided that the best approach to the CIO's request would be to review background information on the industry, the organization, the Information and Management Service's group, and then to review the events of the day, carefully considering the sources of risk.

Industry Background

The commercial and industrial lighting market is dominated by nine companies who together control 50% of the over four billion dollar market. LL is the number one company in the market, having one close competitor in the over $500 million in sales category. In the 1980s, a series of acquisitions and mergers reduced the number of lighting companies, leaving only one-third the number existing in the 1960's. The giants remaining offered a wider variety of lighting products, striving to gain contracts for the entire package of lighting used in a construction project.

The CIO, speaking to a local meeting of the Society for Information Management (SIM), identified four critical success factors for the lighting industry:

> One is product; that is what kinds of products -- a broad or narrow product line -- do we have? Two is price as it relates to the competition. Three is availability; that is, do we make an inventory of standard items available to the local distributors and contractors and how fast can we get our customers

non-standard fixtures from one of our factories as compared to our competitors. Four is service; how do we stack up, one competitor to the other, in the service we give to our customers.

Market entities to be serviced are agents, distributors, specifiers, warehouses, and contractors. Independent agents who employ marketing representatives earn commissions on products sold. They usually have exclusive rights to a company's products within a territory, and can not carry competing products. Agents are the primary interface between the lighting company and the market.

The CIO told the consultant that the idea of using information technology in agencies occurred when he was trying to create an enterprise model. Only when the agent was in the center could he prevent relationship lines from crossing. Agents have gradually assumed many of the roles, particularly that of providing technical expertise, played by the distributors in the 1960's and 1970's. As lighting companies grew larger and offered a wide range of lighting products, the agent became capable of providing the entire job package. Agents define what products are needed for a job, price the products applying their own commissions, and place orders. Agents know the local markets and cultivate relationships with local contractors and specifiers.

The distributor, who had previously assembled a package for a contractor by contacting many agents, now primarily provides readily available inventory and financing to contractors. The contractor awarded the job will then order from an agent or distributor. Stock items are inventoried at independent warehouses, but customized products must be ordered from the company's product divisions.

Once a quote is converted to an order, communication regarding order status and shipping dates is required to effectively schedule labor at the job site. The high degree of coordination required in the construction industry makes information and timely communication of that information a very valuable service. Thus, access to that information gives an agent a competitive advantage.

Company Background

Lithonia Lighting is organized by product group divisions. Three of the six Senior Vice Presidents head product group divisions. The President and the Senior Vice Presidents are known as the "Seniors" or the "Senior Seven." The Chief Information Officer (CIO) role is assigned to a Senior Vice President of one of these product group divisions, Management, Information, and Electronic Systems (M.I.E.S.). In addition to his responsibility for Information and Management Services (I & MS), he is responsible for the Controls, Emergency Systems, and Reloc (relocatable lighting) product divisions. Each of these three areas is headed by a Vice President; thus, the CIO has three direct reports.

The Fluorescent division, founded in Lithonia, Georgia in 1946, is the oldest division and is the world's largest manufacturer of fluorescent lighting fixtures. Its present corporate headquarters is in Conyers, Georgia.

The Hi-Tek division was established in 1971 to capture a new and growing market: high intensity discharge lighting. Begun as a result of a lighting market analysis, the group was led by a manager who had been responsible for Materials Management and Information Systems in Conyers. The present CIO had reported to this manager at that time.

Through new product development and acquisitions, LL came to offer products for most segments of the commercial lighting market. In 1989, LL had 3.3 million square feet of facility space and 13 manufacturing sites in six states and in Canada. Total employment exceeded 5,000 and a large percentage of these employees had been members of the Lithonia Lighting team for over ten years.

Information and Management Services (I& MS) Background

The VP of I & MS, has four direct reports: Director of Data Processing, Director of Information Systems, Manager of Systems Training, and Systems Engineering. Data Processing is responsible for operations, hardware services, and communications. Information systems is responsible for application systems, internally and in the field. Training includes field training for market entities, internal systems training, and a support line for the field and within the company.

Of these four direct reports, two positions were open due to a separation and a resignation.   The CIO had commented that people at LL did not understand how he could have let the Director of Data Processing be separated. He was a well-liked, long-term member of the LL family. The Systems Engineering position had become open during the last month due to a resignation. The manager of systems training position had been open due to turnover, but was filled by promotion from within during the last year.

Prior to a major restructuring in 1989, field system implementation, support, and training reported to a VP of Management Services. The consultant had noted that the former VP of Management Services wore the university ring of the CEO's and CIO's alma mater. He had worked at LL in various capacities since graduating from the university.

Since the restructuring which combined field or agency support and internal system support, this VP had taken responsibility for the new Controls product division. He still reported to the CIO. This VP had a reputation for thoroughness and attention to detail.

After the new product division was created and the information technology unit restructured, both agency support and all other information technology functions reported to the former VP of Information Systems, who was now named the VP of Information and Management Services.

As LL headed toward the $1 billion in sales mark, volumes increased, new systems were added, and old systems enhanced. Many of these systems were mission critical, that is, the company simply could not do business without them. Therefore, the pressures experienced by the I & MS group intensified with the company's growth.

Each market entity's systems were connected through a data communication network called Light*Link. Work on a contractor system, CALL (Contractor Access to Lithonia Lighting) was in progress. The Society for Information Management (SIM) commended LL for Light*Link, a network of personal computers located in 35 warehouses, 84 agent's office, many distributor and specifier offices. The CIO and CEO were awarded the 1988 SIM Partners in Leadership award at the 1988 SIM Annual conference in Minneapolis, Minnesota. Excerpts from the nomination speech follow:

> In 1976, Lithonia Lighting embarked on an explicit strategy of improving its competitive posture -- long before it was popular to talk of using information technology to gain competitive advantage. The central feature of the strategy . . . was to increase sales and profit level by posturing Lithonia in a manner that enabled it to be a company that was "easy to do business with" and to deliver the "best value in lighting" . . . . . During the following seven year period (1981-1988) over which Light*Link evolved, Lithonia invested $5 million and added to its staff individuals with unique expertise in underlying technology critical to the system plan.
>
> Light*Link could not have emerged as an information systems project without the partnership between [the CEO] and [the CIO]. It was not an information systems project, it was a top level, yet fundamental, business strategy. It was a corporate commitment. [The CIO] became the catalyst that forged information technology enabling the firm to pursue its strategy . . . When the Light*Link vision was being created, the quality of data communication services had not yet advanced to

current levels. Vendors were not able to offer adequate business
solutions . . .

[The CIO] recognized early on that personal computers could become an
awesome competitive weapon for Lithonia and its agents if the appropriate
network of support systems were established. The decision and the commitment to proceed occurred before the IBM PC had become the industry
standard (and while many corporate staff members considered PC's to be
nothing more than toys). Personal computers, along with computer networking
became the means of linking agents, specifiers, etc. into the Light*Link system.

Instead of using jargon, Light*Link systems were named with acronyms which made
sense. Agents were provided with an ACE in the marketplace, an Agency Communications Environment for processing orders, determining order status, generating
engineering layouts and calculations. They were also provided agency management
systems, including training for using widely available microcomputer software such as
spreadsheets and word processing. Light*Link bonded the agent to LL and raised
switching costs, or the cost to change to another lighting supplier. Likewise, field
warehouses were given help by SOS, a Stock Order System.

While these field systems were being developed and enhanced (ACE+, SOS+), two
programs for internal systems were begun in the mid '80s. The CIO called these
programs EXCEL(EXcellence through Customer service Emphasis at Lithonia) and
OLA (One Lithonia Architecture). The EXCEL and OLA programs followed
Lithonia's philosophy of continuous improvement at each process in order to stay
ahead of the competition.

The EXCEL program involved the following subsets:
- o   SELL (Sales Environment at Lithonia Lighting)
- o   A2P (Available to Promise)
- o   MILL (Manufacturing Information at Lithonia Lighting)
- o   ESS (Effective Scheduling System)
- o   ROLL (Routing Orders at Lithonia Lighting)
- o   Credit system
- o   BILL (Billing Information at Lithonia Lighting)

OLA's goal was to provide one face to the market for LL, integrating product lines
from different divisions and restructuring existing systems to provide the foundation
needed for a $1 billion sales volume. As volume, products, and product customization
increased, the present hardware and software foundations became increasingly
susceptible to unanticipated problems. A priority was to upgrade the present software
and hardware foundations. Microcomputers in the field were already being replaced
with IBM PS/2's.

LL has worked toward the client server model with the mainframe acting as a central repository and database server while most of the processing is distributed throughout the organization and among market entities. Portions of selected databases would be distributed as well. Extract databases would continue to be used.

The CIO of LL is committed to using information technology to change how companies compete in their market. Speaking before a group of CIO's at a local SIM meeting, he challenged these CIO's to do likewise.

Reviewing the Day's Events

At 8:30 a.m., the CIO went to the conference room adjacent to his office and wrote on the board with a red marker: "Meeting Topic: Improving Performance." He filled his coffee cup and began to pace impatiently, eager for the 8:45 A.M. meeting to begin. Key I & MS staff members, some three levels away from him in the formal structure of the I & MS organization, were to attend.

The CIO began the meeting by pointing to the topic on the board. "We're here to identify measures we can take immediately to improve performance. We have already gained approval to expand mainframe capacity, increasing the number of access channels. This upgrade will be effective in 30 days." He looked around the room, examining each familiar face, gauging the impact of this announcement.

The VP of I & MS had not yet arrived. He continued, "For some months now, I have not been involved in day-to-day operations. Now, I'll be looking at daily performance measures. During the Seniors meeting yesterday, I was told that a distributor in Dothan, Alabama, had switched to another supplier because of the downtime experienced with systems and computers. The Senior VP of Marketing told me that the distribution managers who used facsimile machines to fax orders to agents and to send shipping instructions to warehouses were heroes! They should be given medals for entrepreneurship! At least they were responding when the system wasn't working."

He pauses, waiting for this accusation to sink in, then lowers his voice: "Senior executives are keeping numbers, logs of problems. Their numbers may not be correct and we may not agree with them, but the very fact that they feel the need to keep numbers is a bad indication. They are saying that we are losing business because we can't keep our systems up." There was no sound in the room. He had their attention.

"Our problems are very visible. The business depends on our performance. We know the long term solution: distributed database management using the client server model to reduce mainframe access problems. But in the interim, we can do better, much better. It is the level of expectation which we have created by our own past performance to which we are presently being compared. We're not here to throw blame on anyone, but rather to identify what I'll term responsiveness problems which we can control."

The CIO cited an example. A warehouse microcomputer failed to receive its nightly update for SOS (Stock Order System). The modem continued to try to make a connect all night, resulting in an all night long distance call but no transmission. The CIO asserted that this should never happen. I & MS should be following procedures to monitor transmissions, and he thundered, "respond to a failure like a parent responds to an electrical failure when he has a baby on a iron lung. But maybe kids are like customers. Expendable. Power failure. Throw them away. Have another. File a malfunction report in triplicate."

The manager of the customer support function spoke up: "We've had so many calls lately, more than we can handle. Instead of calling for help, yelling that we have an emergency because we have so many people on hold or call back, we have just become tolerant of customers having to wait to talk to us. We've just become tolerant of all the lines being busy -- what we don't get to today, we'll get to tomorrow. We may need some help until some of the problems causing calls are resolved, but we can get our attitudes about problem calls straightened out."

The CIO nodded, "Good," and looked around the room for further discussion. "What mainframe performance measures are we reacting to?" Since the Data Processing Director position was open, he looked to the operations manager, who had been on the job only a few weeks. The operations manager identified a weekly report. The CIO expanded on the iron lung analogy. "You mean the kid has been dead for a week before you know it?" The operations manager admitted that he was really responding to customer complaints. "You mean you're reacting to the kid screaming. We should know the power went out before he does. I want you to identify your pulse points, the places to monitor so that problems can be intercepted. Then use measures of these pulse points as a basis for action," the CIO paused.

The VP of I&MS arrived, and slumped down in his chair. He looked tired. The VP pointed out that the connect problem, the reasons for modems hanging up, was a Novell Netware problem. He complained that Novell was mainly a marketing company with little technical assistance. The CIO responded that systems software could be written to compensate for this problem with Netware: "Can you think of a better use of that time? When the connect is not made, we suffer in the market."

Then he looked up and asked quietly, "Where is the SOS machine located now? Who sits beside it to know when modem lights are not blinking, when the screen delivers an error message?" The VP of I& MS responded that it was currently in a room by itself because of vacation time granted.

After a short coffee break, the CIO reiterated, "We must take very visible and effective action now. For us, the customer -- the agent, the distributor, the warehouse -- is our baby in an iron lung. Two items remain on the agenda: eliminating the faxing of orders now and formulating a plan to present our systems to a major new opportunity for business.

So, why are our customers in the fax business anyway?" The VP responded, his Northern accent indicating that he was not one of the local hires. He had been recruited from a copy machine company, with one of his strong points considered to be his technical competence. "When the mainframe is down or there is partial availability, orders cannot be processed. Product availability must be confirmed and inventory allocated to process the orders. This requires the mainframe's inventory database. If the mainframe is down, the order is not processed and no bill of lading is created for the distribution center or warehouse to ship the product. Distribution centers faxed copies of the order to the warehouse so that the warehouse could use the paper order to assemble and then ship the order."

The CIO listened patiently and then added, "So orders are shipped from inventory which may have been allocated to another customer and inventory is depleted without changing the inventory database and thus the manufacturing schedule. Correct?" The CIO's second in command, the VP of Information and Management Services, paused and replied, "Yes, sir."

"During the meeting today we're looking at both sides of the coin. At the same time that our systems are causing critical problems, we are proposing them as the key factor in our marketing strategy for a major new opportunity. We have a major customer who is currently doing $12 million in sales with us annually. They have decided to use one source for lighting, which will mean $30-40 million in business with the prospect of this amount increasing to $100 million. They've looked at all the major lighting companies and settled on two, one of which is Lithonia Lighting."

"Despite the performance problems experienced lately, the Seniors all agreed yesterday that our systems are our main competitive advantage in this situation. We can install the distributor system (DIAL-L) at the customer site and let the customer enter orders, confirm orders, and check order status. The seniors agreed that this service and quick turn around on orders is what we can do that our major competitor can't do. I want you to leave with things in perspective. Our systems are critical. They provide a competitive advantage no one else has. Thus, it's urgent to fix failures."

Following the meeting, the CIO interviewed two applicants, one for a micro engineering position and the other for the critical job of Technical Services Manager. The Technical Services Manager applicant had been with the same company for twenty years. In his last position there, he had been responsible for operations and technical services. After his children left home, he and his wife decided to look for a challenge and a change. He had not regretted the move to Atlanta. Both he and his wife liked Atlanta, and he had enjoyed the opportunity to work with new technology, even though he had been among those included in a massive reduction in force at the high tech firm.

During the interview, the CIO confided in the applicant that he was very concerned about the I & MS group. He also confided that he had hoped to retire in three years. After investing twenty-four years in the organization, he wanted to be sure the competitive advantage provided by information technology would be sustained and not backfire, as it seemed to have done in the last few months.

He asked the applicant if the VP of I & MS had told him about the turnover problem among the technical staff. The applicant nodded, but seemed interested in hearing the CIO's reasons. The CIO continued, "We made a decision that the Data Processing Director was not a good fit for the pressures accompanying a $1 billion sales volume, which is where we're heading. He was a well-liked member of the Lithonia family. Some of our technical people decided to leave as well."

The applicant responded that the VP of Information and Management Services had given him two goals for the open position: (1) rebuild the computer operations staff and (2) stabilize technical services. The CIO hastened to add a third goal: provide a high level of customer service. "We're about lighting not about computers. If you were hired, we'd make a lighting business man out of you first and a computer person second-- send you to school on lighting, teach you to calculate the appropriate lighting for a room, be sure you understand our products and how our customers work on a day-to-day basis."

The applicant nodded and replied: "I've been to the library to read what I could find about Lithonia Lighting. I read the article where you said that we had to know the business, not run around like 'three headed yo-yos serving the data processing god.'" The applicant laughed. He had enjoyed that article. "What I've read is one of the reasons I've stayed interested in the job. I know getting along with one's boss is important. So I've spent enough time with the VP to feel comfortable about working for him. I've explained that I like to work within guidelines, but want the 'how' to be left to me. I think most technical people need a certain autonomy." The CIO nodded.

The CIO was scheduled to deliver a speech before the parent company's Board of Directors Saturday morning. Following the interviews, he previewed the speech and visual aids to accompany the speech for the CEO. The topic was the Management, Information, and Electronics Services (M.I.E.S.) division.

The CEO listened closely and many details were changed. He liked the presentation, but seemed concerned. After the preview, the CIO told him that he would meet with the Senior VP of Marketing and of Sales this afternoon concerning their discussion yesterday. He also told him that the staff meeting this morning had been productive and watched his friend's face carefully. The CEO simply responded, "Good."

The CIO began the meeting with the Senior VP of Marketing and Senior VP of Sales by saying that the problems being experienced were his fault. Because of the plan to use distributed processing, upgrades to the mainframe had been delayed. An upgrade was scheduled for installation within the next thirty days. Response time would improve and less downtime would be experienced with order processing. The Senior VP of Sales responded enthusiastically, "Boy, Charlie, that's great. Thirty days you say," and made a note in his calendar. "You know, until we talked last night, I had no idea how important these phone lines are, too."

The VP of I& MS, spoke up, "I want you guys to know that we're working on one cause of terminals hanging up." He explained the problem with locked records when more than two agents try to check order status on one record and he explained the work now being done to correct the problem.

The CIO smiled. "Now we've got to stop building Towers of Babylon with fax machines! We can't keep the mainframe from ever going down or prevent all connect problems. But we can give distributors and agents who are going down the ability to print entered but unconfirmed orders when problems occur. The Los Angeles Distribution Center should be our first target." The VP of Sales nodded briskly.

The CIO explained that the use of printers would be enhanced over time, allowing customers to select ranges of orders to print or just one order. But the print-out in a rough, usable form would be available Tuesday. The mood of the meeting shifted as the CIO's responsiveness became evident. The Senior VP of Sales said, "Charlie, this is great. Appreciate it," and stood up to leave. The Senior VP of Marketing shook hands with the CIO, "We can live with this, Charlie. Thanks."

The VP of I & MS stayed over to tell the CIO that the systems program to bypass Novell's Netware connect problems could be ready in two weeks if the systems programmer did nothing else. The CIO responded, "Can you think of a better use of this resource now? Two weeks, then." He added, "I'm for hiring the applicant for the Data Processing Director job." They discussed the offer to be made.

A Recommendation

The consultant leaned back in her chair, looked into the pool of light on her desk, and began to reflect on what the CIO must do to be able to retire in three years. What must he do to reduce the risks without sacrificing the rewards of using information technology for competitive advantage? Clearly, the two questions were related. The consultant knew that background information by itself would not have been sufficient to separate the problems from symptoms of problems. Experience in the organization had provided an understanding of the situation which could not have been gained from interviews or analysis of financial data.

EXERCISE

1.   Compare the work life of a CIO doing "bread and butter" applications and that of the Lithonia Lighting CIO.

2.   What do you think it would be like to work at Lithonia Lighting in the I & MS division? Consider personal relationships, job security, challenges, opportunities for advancement and development.

3.   Why did LL give priority to market entities when developing systems rather than first developing internal systems?

4.   What are the advantages of the CIO having responsibility for product divisions? the disadvantages?

5.   Support the statement, "The CIO is a skilled communicator," using specific examples from the case.

6.   What is the "bottleneck" in the Light*Link network?

7.   How important is the CIO's familiar relationship with other senior executives? What factors contribute to this familiarity?

8.   Do you agree with the CIO's recommendation on the Director applicant? Why? Cite specific reasons from the case.

9.   List reasons for the current crisis. What situations or events have led to the current crisis? Remember that positive situations and events can precipitate a crisis.

CASE 23
YOUNG WORKERS BAKERY[1]

Being a supplier in supermarket strategic information systems is the last thing Jo Irving imagined would happen to the Young Workers Bakery (YWB). While talking in the quiet back booth in a dimly lit local cafe one day in the summer of 1989, she was asked, in her opinion, why her bakery was in business? She thought for a moment, then stated with simple sincerity, "To make a good loaf of bread." Jo is one of four collective owners ("the members") of YWB, a whole grain bakery located in a previously run-down and recently fashionable section of downtown Buffalo.

The YWB was started in 1976 to make both a political statement and a good loaf of bread while providing an environment in which people who were uncomfortable in a traditional corporate structure could earn a decent living. The structure of six people (three female and three male) working together informally and equally underwent some changes as members came and went. There have been 20 members over the bakery's history. All of the members are "full time". They work 8 hours per day, 4 days per week. In addition, they all attend a weekly meeting which deals with day to day operations of the bakery. These meetings discuss ways of improving the production process, efficiency, the quality of the supplies and any personal information. There are also monthly planning meetings at which long term goals are discussed.

As of 1985 the bakery has had "employees" who work at the bakery but do not have any ownership rights. The employees are all more or less part time. They do not

---

[1]   This case was prepared by Coral R. Snodgrass, Gerald S. Rosenfelder, and Edward J. Szewczak, Canisius College.

attend the weekly and monthly meetings. The members are experimenting with ways to get the employees involved in meetings. The most appealing alternative is to have the employees meet with the members on paid time. Given the members' value system, it is important to them to have the employees and the members all participate in the decision making process. The decision to have employees was a difficult one for the members to make. They required a steady, reliable work force and they had a number of good people who were happy to work for them but who wanted none of the responsibilities of ownership. At present there are four members, six employees and a computer analyst. Of the four members, three have been there 5 years and one (Jo) has been there 11 years. The computer analyst was one of YWB's most recent hires.

The decision making at YWB is not cost driven. It is worker driven. One of the founding values of the bakery which has not changed is the goal of providing people with a decent living in an atmosphere of openness and mutual respect. Consequently, job scheduling is done around individuals' needs, such as scheduling for day care. The jobs rotate from day to day. And even though some individuals have become specialized through skills and experience with certain tasks, people can still do whatever task they want, provided the bakery goods are produced. One developing exception to this has emerged in the area of sales where the computer analyst has become the predominant "sales person". This change has come about because of the nature of the market and the need to deal with that market in a uniform fashion. But it is still true that, with this one exception, titles are merely nominal and the structure is egalitarian. Power is shared along with responsibility. For the members of YWB, the value for the growth of the individuals is as important as the bread.

Because individual growth and support are so important, growth in sales has been used to support increased benefits for the members and the employees. As the needs of the people changed, so have the benefits. There is support for child care and for health insurance. There are paid vacations in addition to the unpaid ones they always had. In order to be sure that the bakery and the people are growing together, members have frequent meetings. There are weekly meetings to discuss general issues that people have put on the agenda. There are meetings away from the bakery where they discuss long term goals. They also have social get togethers. Because this personal interaction is so important, screening new people is vital. Anyone who wants to be a member of the collective must first go through an apprenticeship. During this period, they attend all the meetings but they have no voting rights. After this probationary period, the members vote on admission into the collective. Employees only have to serve an apprenticeship if they desire to become members. Such care about the interactions of the members and employees has helped to sustain the bakery through all of its years of operation.

At present, the members of the bakery are at a crossroads. Growing awareness of the dangers of environmental pollution and a growing concern with health issues have made the pure products of YWB very popular with a wide spectrum of consumers. There is the possibility of substantial growth. However, the very concept of such growth poses a challenge to the members' fundamental values for a cooperative, flexible, informal work place. In addition, the value system of the members is such that they have generally used excess profits to improve the benefits for their workers, not to support growth. Although the members do not believe a decision must be made immediately, there is a sense that the bakery is "riding the crest" of society's new concern for the environment and the members need to define for themselves how they want to be a part of this.

The Pre-Supermarket Era

When YWB opened, local cooperatives were the main outlets, accounting for 98% of sales. The bakery also sold to a few health food stores. At that time YWB had a policy of not selling to supermarkets. To the members such markets were the embodiment of a corrupt food system, which exploited the relationships between the consumer, the employee and the environment. It was precisely from such a system that YWB wanted to break away. The members' values were for a cooperative, interactive relationship that integrated quality supplies, participative decision making, concern for the environment and the provision of pure foods at a reasonable price. The product line at that time was fairly simple. It consisted mainly of organic whole wheat bread with some cookies, muffins and specialty items.

From the beginning, everything at YWB was informal and everything was done as simply as possible. Its technology was "low tech". The dough was kneaded by hand. The food was packaged in simple wrappers and deliveries were made from the back of a station wagon. The members never budgeted for advertising. They relied on word-of-mouth advertising. Economics dictated that YWB not spend lavishly. However, the members' value systems would have called for such simplicity in any event. Their values for the bakery and its product line were part of the "politics of food". As a political statement, they wanted to make nutritional food with as few chemicals and pollutants as possible. Further, they would not engage in behaviors which they believed to be "inappropriate behaviors" such as advertising or merchandising. Kneading the dough by hand was done not just because a dough mixer was expensive. The members did it because kneading the dough by hand gave them a "spiritual" connection with their products.

However YWB's members understood the need to be flexible in order to insure the survival of the bakery. As an example, although the members felt very strongly that they did not want to become alienated from their products, they recognized that some things had to become mechanized. Kneading the dough by hand is difficult and exhausting work. At first the members purchased a dough mixer for $300, but the mixer has proven inadequate given the level of demand for bakery products. However, adequate mixers cost between $5,000 and $10,000, and the members have not come to a consensus on the purchase of a new mixer. Some other steps in the production process are also tedious and unfulfilling. One such step is wrapping the products. Although this is now done by hand, the members believe that acquiring a packaging machine would be an appropriate use of resources. But they know intuitively that production volume is insufficient to make such a purchase cost effective. They do not know for certain what the break even point would be for such a purchase.

As another example, very early on YWB had problems with the consistency of both the quality and the quantity of the supply of organic flour. In addition to the problem of a consistent supply is the problem of costs. Organic flour is very expensive. The members have established a product line which is about half organic and half non-organic. However, they only use whole grain flour.

The product line has expanded to include approximately 47 different items. Eight products account for 74% of sales volume (Table 1). The staple of the product line is and always has been whole wheat bread which constitutes 20% of their sales volume. This is made with non-organic flour. Another 6% of sales comes from organic whole wheat bread.

Table 1
Top Eight Products by Dollars of Sales Volume

PRODUCT NAME	PERCENTAGE OF SALES DOLLARS
Whole Wheat Bread	20
Oatmeal Raisin Cookies	12
Three Seed Bread	11
Oat Bran Muffins	8
Granola	7
Organic Whole Wheat	6
Oat Sunflower Cookies	6
Bran Muffins	4

Changes to the product line come from experimentation at the bakery, from recipes acquired through a nationwide cooperative network, and from customer suggestions.

YWB produces a selection of products which are free of eggs, dairy products, salt, yeast and wheat. Any changes to the product line must fit into the members value set and this is not always easy. As an example, in 1989 there was a great deal of national media attention given to oat bran because of studies showing the beneficial effects of oat bran on cholesterol. Consequently there was a great demand for oat bran in various forms. Because of the bakery's production flexibility and the fact they had already been doing some experimentation, YWB was in a position to begin production of oat bran muffins very quickly. It might seem that this is a marketer's dream -- a product which has been shown to be healthful and for which there is now a tremendous demand and which could quickly be brought into production. YWB should simply launch into production and take advantage of the trend. But the members of YWB did not see it that way. They were concerned that introducing oat bran muffins might be a form of exploitation of a media event. They took the time to explore the ramifications of their decisions and to determine the appropriateness of what they were doing. YWB did decide to begin production of oat bran muffins, but only after the members were sure that the decision was in congruence with their value system. They produced oat bran muffins because one of their values is to be especially responsive to the dietary needs of their customers.

The customer base has grown over the years and covers a wide variety of people who are attracted to YWB for a number of reasons. Some customers have allergies or other health problems and they are seeking foods that will not harm them. Some are athletes who are seeking the high carbohydrate, sugar-free, no cholesterol foods. There are senior citizens who are concerned about their health. Many of the customers are students. There are still some customers who are "food political" such as some vegetarians. Some customers come for the fad. The members of the bakery themselves do not have a profile of their "typical customer" except to say that the typical customer is a health conscious, "main stream" person who wants a healthful product and is willing to pay for it.

YWB products typically cost 50% more than similar supermarket foods. As an example, four YWB oat bran muffins cost $1.89. A package of six store brand muffins (complete with chemicals and preservatives) costs $1.69. The two packages sit side by side on the shelf and customers buy out the YWB goods daily. In April, 1989 increased costs prompted YWB to raise prices as much as 50% on some products. There was no immediate decrease in demand. The demand and the customer base appear to be not only sustainable but capable of growth. Even though the products are considerably more expensive than the supermarket brands, they compare quite favorably with premium national brands, especially when the contents are considered. In addition, YWB compares favorably with other bakeries. As an example, YWB produces both a pecan and a pumpkin pie. Each pie sells for $8.30. Two other local bakeries also make pecan and pumpkin pies and they also claim to use pure ingredients. One bakery charges $9.50 for the pecan pie and $7.50 for the pumpkin pie. Another bakery charges $8.95 for a large pie and $6.95 for a small one.

There is no doubt that the YWB product line is quite popular. The bakery has seen constant increases in sales even though the members do not advertise and they do no marketing. One of the reasons that the bakery has seen no decline in demand is the fact that it has no direct competition.   Few bakeries offer organic products. Non-organic bakeries which use processed sugar and flour are not perceived as direct competition. The customer who buys from YWB is not looking for just any loaf of bread.

The niche that YWB enjoys in the market is unique, but it is not a particularly profitable one.   In addition, at the present scale of operations, the existing cost structure is not expected to change. Consequently, it is not expected that new competitors will emerge to take advantage of lower production costs.

The Supermarket Era

YWB's customer base has been growing steadily, and its distribution channels have been changing. There is very little retail done at the bakery itself. YWB has 43 outlets to supply with bakery goods. Whereas the co-ops were the main outlets, they now account for only 25% of sales. The other 75% comes from supermarkets and convenience stores.

Within the past two years, supermarkets have approached YWB for its products. This development prompted some changes at the bakery in terms of personnel, the development of new recipes, and technology. The changes came about because of the way large stores do business. Such stores pay by check and they pay on longer time schedules.   Consequently the bakery had to have a way to keep good records, something it had never had to pay much attention to in the past. Secondly, the bakery needed to have some control over its finances. All of the financial decisions were made by the members together. But the increases in sales have made control of the relevant financial data more difficult. Consequently, the members hired a computer analyst to computerize their financial statements. The analyst (the husband of a member) recommended the purchase of a personal computer and the members approved his request.

The shift to the supermarkets also forced the bakery to formalize its product line. Because supermarkets have their own product lines and prices computerized, they require a stable supply of products. They also require at least three weeks to put a new product into their computer. Once it is in there, they do not want to have to change it. They also require UPC bar codes on all products which are scanned at checkout.

The stabilization of the product line has not been a welcomed change for the bakery because it has limited the amount of experimentation the members can do. Furthermore, the products they do develop must be more carefully chosen so as not to conflict with supermarket requirements. The members still do some experimentation and they use the co-ops as outlets for the new products. But in many ways the change to using the supermarkets has heavily constrained their freedom to experiment.

In the pre-supermarket era, members often produced new products and delivered them to co-ops in small batches to see how well they would be received by customers. If the product did not sell, then the members concluded that the experiment was a failure and the product was not produced again. The cost of such experiments was low and no consideration of lead times was necessary. If the product was successful, larger batches could be produced and distributed at will. No product coding was required. In the supermarket era, things have become more formalized both in terms of developing and distributing products and in the interactions with supermarket personnel. Products must be registered at least three weeks in advance and bar codes assigned. Also YWB's product lists are evaluated by supermarkets in terms of their own requirements, which are not always fully understood by YWB members. At one supermarket, the purchasing manager appeared to treat YWB's offering of products whimsically, picking and choosing items seemingly at random. In addition, YWB was unable to collect data on the types of people who were purchasing YWB products, though they believed that the supermarkets were able to collect this data as part of the checkout scanning process.

To deal with the more formalized way of doing business, the members agreed to allow the computer analyst to be the liaison between YWB and the supermarkets. After all, the personal computer he had recommended appeared to be fully satisfactory in meeting YWB's needs and even proved useful in developing programs for pricing YWB's products. And of all YWB people he was most familiar with information technology.

However, over a period of time, some of the members began to view the computer analyst's style as brusque and somewhat intolerant. For example, when the idea was suggested that YWB find some way to develop customer profiles from the data collected routinely by the supermarkets, the computer analyst belittled the idea as not useful but did not fully explain why he felt this way.

The members generally have found that consensus is harder to achieve in the supermarket era. The computer analyst is perceived by some of the members as partly responsible for this. Some view him as "power hungry", autocratic, and wanting to "manage". Some members resent his "specialist" attitude and accuse him of not doing the hard work of baking expected of all members and employees. Even though the computer analyst is married to a member, he is not wanted as a member by the other members.

The Future

Growth for YWB has been slow and natural. As the bakery has grown, change has been absorbed gradually and without trauma. Until now, the informal, egalitarian structure of the business has not been threatened. Though the prospects for continued growth as a supplier to supermarkets look favorable, Jo Irving will not be participating in this anticipated growth. She left YWB at the beginning of 1991.

EXERCISE

1.   Can YWB really expect to grow given their limited resources and member control of the organization? Is the members' value system consistent with growth?

2.   How would you describe the members perception of the value of information technology? Do you see the possibility of YWB developing an information technology strategy in the near future? What would be necessary before such a strategy could be successfully articulated?

3.   In the face of economic necessity, YWB agreed to become a supplier to supermarkets. What changes occurred at YWB in light of this agreement? Were these changes for the better? Explain.

4.   The computer analyst is not very popular at YWB. Is this the result of his being incompetent? If the computer analyst is not incompetent, then what factors are at work which account for the friction and resentment he is creating?